AUGUSTINE

the

EVANGELIST

The Zeal, Hope and Methodology
of the Bishop of Hippo

Ryan Denton

Foreword Thomas J. Nettles, PhD

A publication of

THE
Greater Heritage
Sound Theology · *Intellectual Rigor*
Winter Springs, FL

Augustine the Evangelist: The Zeal, Hope and Methodology of the Bishop of Hippo by Ryan Denton
This paperback and eBook edition first published in January 2022
© 2022 by Ryan Denton

Published by The Greater Heritage
                1170 Tree Swallow Dr., Suite 309
                Winter Springs, FL 32708

Email: info@thegreaterheritage.com
Website: www.thegreaterheritage.com

Cover Design: J.R. Waller
Cover Image: *The Roman Theater at Taormina*, 1828 by Louise-Joséphine Sarazin de Belmont (painter) French, 1790 - 1870. The National Gallery of Art, Washington, DC. Gift of Frank Anderson Trapp. 2004.166.33.
Font(s): Adobe Caslon Pro, Gill Sans Nova, Haboro, Vollkorn.

ISBN (paperback): 978-1-953855-60-2
ISBN (PDF): 978-1-953855-64-0
ISBN (EPUB): 978-1-953855-65-7

1 2 3 4 5 6 7 8 9 10   26 25 24 23 22

"As life in the Western world increasingly bears parallels to life in the late Roman Empire, Augustine of Hippo's life and ministry engage us with fresh relevance. In this concise volume, Ryan Denton introduces us to Augustine the Evangelist. This is a great story of a man with an evangelical heart in action, but even more marvelously, it is a narrative of our Lord Jesus Christ saving and sanctifying a sinner from another time and culture to become an instrument for the salvation and sanctification of many others. What Christ did then, he continues to call us into, and do, today."

> **Dr. William Vandoodewaard**, PhD, Professor, Puritan Reformed Theological Seminary, author of *The Quest for the Historical Adam: Genesis, Hermeneutics, and Human Origins*

"Despite my own interest in both theology and evangelism, I had never viewed Augustine as an evangelist. I am grateful to Ryan Denton for this carefully researched and clearly written book which demonstrated the evangelistic zeal of this great church father. James Denney once quipped, "If our evangelists were theologians and our theologians were evangelists, we would be near the ideal church." Denton's work will challenge and inspire you to be more faithful in the task of the Great Commission."

> **Dr. Timothy K. Beougher,** Associate Dean, Billy Graham School of Missions, Evangelism and Ministry; Professor of Evangelism and Church Growth, The Southern Baptist Theological Seminary

"Academics have regularly studied Augustine the theologian, the polemicist, the rhetorician, the linguist, and the progenitor of semiotics, but few have expounded on Augustine the pastor and evangelist. Strategically drawing from Augustine's cultural context and sermons, Ryan Denton's book offers an unvarnished view of Augustine as evangelist. Denton serves the reader well by quoting Augustine's sermons as primary evidence, by not sugar-coating the struggles Augustine has about various means of conversions, but also by showing the pastoral heart of a man who is willing to travel out of his way in order to facilitate a conversion. For those of us who greatly admire Augustine the theologian—this book challenges us to imitate Augustine the evangelist."

> **Dr. Mark Gring,** Associate Professor and Chair, Communication Studies Department, Texas Tech University

"Augustine of Hippo a passionate evangelist? Indeed! In this excellent work author Ryan Denton plainly establishes this fact. Educational and exciting, this volume motivates us to follow in the footsteps of this great theologian who earnestly preached Christ to the lost. I highly encourage everyone to "take up and read" this book."

> **Pastor Rob Ventura,** Grace Community Baptist Church, North Providence, Rhode Island, co-author of *A Portrait of Paul* and *Spiritual Warfare*

"After having already been immensely blessed and challenged by Denton's *Even if None*, I warmly recommend his newest work, Augustine the Evangelist. I knew there was much to learn from Augustine, but this book opens up a whole new perspective that is bound to be a great encouragement to Christians today. It is so much more than just an analysis of the church father's views on and practice of evangelism. It drips with gospel-optimism which is so desperately needed in our day and age of gloom and defeatism. What a refreshing and edifying read!"

> **Dr. Sacha Walicord,** Pastor at Walker United Reformed Church, Grand Rapids, Michigan

Augustine the Evangelist

For my sons

O good God, what happens in a man to make him rejoice more at the salvation of a soul that has been despaired of and then delivered from danger, than over one who has never lost hope, or never been in such imminent danger?

-Augustine, *Confessions*, Book 8, Chapter 3

contents

Dr. Tom J. Nettles

"Thou movest us to delight in praising Thee; for Thou hast formed us for Thyself, and our hearts are restless till they find rest in Thee." So Augustine wrote in book one, chapter one of the Confessions. This knowledge of being made for God, being pursued by God, and of the restless heart until redemption accomplished its work in the sinner drove Augustine to spend his life working for the conversion of sinners and the Christianizing of culture. He preached, wrote, and counseled to that end.

Ryan Denton has given us a succinct and compelling glance at the evangelistic drive of Augustine in his practical ministry and in his theological reasoning. He points out the missteps that had destructive consequences, but does not, for the sake of mistakes, dishonor the honestly Christian spiritual energy and massively positive influence of the Bishop of Hippo.

Denton writes, "His evangelistic shortcomings are vastly outweighed by his achievements, however. Perhaps the greatest achievement is his unwavering optimism in the power of God to save sinners and build up His church." No Christian theologian has affected Western society in as pervasive and comprehensive a way as did Augustine. The inescapable impact of his powers of thought ungenerously highlights the corrosive effects of his mistakes. As in the case of all sinners, however, the good should not be interred with his bones but seen as a special gift of divine grace and merciful provision for escape from the wrath to come. Denton has done this with clarity in the case of Augustine's evangelistic compulsion.

-Dr. Tom J. Nettles, Senior Professor at The Southern Baptist Theological Seminary

Augustine of Hippo has been thought of as many things throughout church history. He is one of the greatest philosophers the West has ever produced: of the same caliber as a Plato, Aristotle, or Kant. He is perhaps the greatest theologian outside of the Bible, with both Roman Catholics and Protestants claiming him as their own. His literary output was so prodigious it would be impossible to read everything he wrote in one lifetime.[1] As a friend and bishop, it would be difficult to find someone more devoted to his duties.

Augustine is typically not thought of as an evangelist, however. In fact, early church history has typically given that title to another Augustine, the one from Canterbury (d. 604). Without taking anything away from Augustine of Canterbury—who did see enormous amounts of converts in present-day England—the moniker "evangelist" must go to

---

[1] It is estimated he wrote 5.4 million words during his ministry. One medieval monk quipped, "He who says he has read all of Augustine...lies!" Speaking of Augustine's works, his contemporary biographer Possidius says, "Scarcely any student would be able to read and know them all." *Life of St. Augustine*, Ch. 18.

the Augustine from Hippo, as well. As we will see, much of Augustine of Hippo's energies were spent engaging the lost through sermons, letters, public debates, books, and personal conversation. His evangelism was not perfect, but he was sincere, and even his sloppiness is preferable to much that passes for evangelism in our day. What is certain is he labored to convert people to God, and he did so with immense success.

This book will explore the methodology of Augustine's evangelism, including the more controversial aspects of predestination, religious coercion, and miracles. It will conclude with a look at Augustine's mastery of experiential preaching and the similarities between his style and later evangelists such as George Whitefield and Puritans such as William Perkins. What emerges is a glimpse of a minister dedicated to the advance of the gospel, despite innumerable challenges and a crumbling Roman Empire.

Why Study Augustine's Evangelism?

The study of Augustine the evangelist is invaluable for the church today, with things to learn both from Augustine's victories and failures. Perhaps the most valuable benefit of such a study is that Augustine's setting was very much like the twenty-first century West. Sexual immorality, paganism, cults, heretics, and a general feeling of malaise marked Augustine's world. He describes the mindset of the Roman Empire in his day as follows: "Let us erect houses of the largest and most ornate description: in these let there be provided the most sumptuous banquets, where every one who pleases may, by day or night, play, drink, vomit, dissipate. Let there be everywhere heard the rustling of dancers, the loud, immodest laughter of the theater; let a succession of the most cruel and the most voluptuous pleasures maintain a perpetual excitement. If such happiness is distasteful to any, let him be branded as a public enemy; and if any attempt to modify or put an end

4

to it, let him be silenced, banished, put an end to."[2]

This is the context in which Augustine labored, and for those living in the contemporary West, it is our context as well. The more historians dig up of Augustine's culture, the more it becomes clear that there is ample overlap between his setting and ours—far more so than even the early Reformers, Puritans, or the era of the Great Awakenings. The purpose of this book is not merely to learn about Augustine the evangelist, but also to apply his approaches to our own context, lives, and ministries. Much of the work done on Augustine has focused on his internal reform of the Christian church. But until we appreciate the evangelistic side of Augustine, our understanding of the man and his ministry will be incomplete. As important as Augustine's internal reform of the church is, our neglect of his external ministries has deprived us of one of the best historical examples for engaging a culture such as ours with the gospel.

Also, despite the resurgence taking place among the Reformed community, there is still a need for a more robustly Reformed approach to evangelism. Material on Reformed evangelism pales in comparison to the synergistic information still popular today. By looking at the roots of Reformed evangelism in the person and ministry of Augustine of Hippo, this book seeks to demonstrate the importance of having a correct theology when sharing the gospel with the lost. What better way to appreciate Reformed evangelism than by studying the man who helped jumpstart it over a thousand years ago, and whose example and writings still have practical relevance in our own era of the church?

Studying Augustine's evangelism methodology will likewise dispel the myth that Reformed theology doesn't encourage missionary zeal. In particular, the study of Augustine is critical if we are to appreciate how

---

2 *City of God*, 2.20.

predestination, the sovereignty of God in conversion, and the free offer of the gospel go hand in hand, not only biblically, which is primary, but also historically. If this can be established in the life and ministry of Augustine, we should expect to see it also in the ministries of those who would later hold these same doctrinal truths—Calvin, Luther, the Puritans, and other Reformers and Post-Reformers—which is exactly what we find. In fact, it would be difficult to fully appreciate the evangelistic methodologies of Calvin, Luther, and the Puritans without a sturdy understanding of Augustine's own methods and views on the same subject.

Recent scholarship is at last appreciating the evangelistic fervor of the Protestant Reformation,[3] but in many respects the Reformers and Post-Reformers were building on the foundation laid by Augustine of Hippo. Perry Miller has said Augustine was more popular than even the Reformers among Puritan readers.[4] William Perkins explicitly acknowledges that his *Arte of Prophesying* was heavily influenced by Augustine's *On Christian Doctrine*.[5] John Calvin famously proclaimed, "Augustinus...totus noster est" ("Augustine is totally ours"). It was said of John Knox that his favorite church fathers were "Augustine and Chrysostom."[6] As inundated as these men were in the works of Augustine, they undoubtedly caught some of his missionary fire. This is why the following study of Augustine is so consequential. If we are to appreciate the militant advance of the gospel in the Reformation and

---

3 To name but two sources, see Michael A. G. Haykin and Jefferey Robinson Sr., *To the Ends of the Earth: Calvin's Missional Vision and Legacy* (Wheaton, IL: Crossway, 2014); Ray Van Neste, "Correcting the Record," *Sixteenth-Century Mission: Explorations in Protestant and Roman Catholic Theology and Practice*, Ed. By Robert L. Gallagher and Edward L. Smither (Bellingham, WA: Lexham Press, 2021).

4 Perry Miller, *The New England Mind: The Seventeenth Century* (Cambridge, MA: Harvard University Press, 1954), 93.

5 Ann-Stephane Schäfer, *Auctoritas Patrum? The Reception of Church Fathers in Puritanism* (Mainz: Peter Lang, 2012), 227.

6 David F. Wright, "John Knox and the Early Church Fathers," *John Knox and the British Reformations* (England: Ashgate Publishing, 1998), 107.

Post-Reformation eras, it is imperative to see the continuity between Augustine's own evangelistic zeal and methodology and that which was produced in sixteenth and seventeenth century Protestant Europe and North America.

Who Is This Book For?

This book is written for any Christian who desires to learn more about Augustine of Hippo, and particularly how one of church history's most towering evangelists went about converting the lost. It will be especially encouraging to pastors who seek to do the work of the evangelist in a more effective way. Church historians will also benefit by seeing a side of Augustine often underappreciated and more rarely written about. This book seeks to correct the imbalance of overlooking such a crucial part of Augustine's ministry while at the same time stoking our zeal to imitate Augustine the evangelist as he imitated Christ.

Augustine was an evangelist who was motivated by the sovereignty of God in salvation. He was a man who believed in an optimistic gospel, knowing that Christ rules and reigns not only in the future, but today, and that the gospel will build up God's church throughout the ages. He was a precursor for evangelistic preaching and presuppositional apologetics. He also made mistakes in his evangelism, such as his views on the miraculous and especially his approaches to religious coercion. Through both his better qualities and mistakes, Augustine offers much to the contemporary Christian to learn from. May the Lord use this book to that end, for His glory alone.

As far as I know, this is the first book-length project devoted exclusively to Augustine's evangelism methodology. Aside from Augustine's sermons, letters, and writings, I have tried to keep abreast of the contemporary research being done on Augustine, most especially in books, scholarly journals, and articles. In deference to the expertise and labor of such scholars, I have included copious amounts of citations in this work but believe it to be a strength rather than a distraction. As much as I appreciate original thought, and there is plenty of that here, I am also aware that scholars of Augustine have spent more time with him. They have soaked in his life and work to a far greater extent than I have. It has been a chief occupation of mine to present Augustine not only in a sympathetic light, but an accurate one. I didn't want to mold Augustine into a distortion that is not Augustine, even if it would fit my desired narrative.

Special thanks to the many readers who offered suggestions and critique as the manuscript developed. The Christian life should never be done in isolation from the community of saints, and the same is certainly true when it comes to the writing of books.

one

Augustine's Conversion and Legacy

To understand Augustine's evangelism, it is necessary to be reminded he lived over fifteen hundred years ago, from 354 - 430 A.D. He spoke and wrote in Latin. He ministered in North Africa. It would be easy to evaluate him according to our idea of missions and evangelism, but this would miss the mark. Although many aspects of his evangelism will be recognizable to the modern reader, much of it will seem foreign and inappropriate. Augustine never used the word "evangelism" in his writings. No one of that time did. There were no missionary societies. There were no conferences or even prayer meetings devoted to un-reached people groups. But this is not to say evangelism and missions was not in the forefront of Augustine's labors.

Augustine was born to a pagan father and Christian mother. As a young man he developed a passion for learning which led him to study various philosophies. He was a follower of Manicheanism and Neoplatonism before being converted to Christianity at 31.[1] By

---

1 Both terms are defined and described in chapter 2.

this time, he was a professor of rhetoric in Milan, one of the most prestigious academic positions in the Roman world. After Augustine was converted, he left his professorship to devote himself to a kind of informal monasticism, surrounded by fellow recluses. They spent their days praying, reading, discussing spiritual themes—a life of "evangelic death" to the business of the world.[2] And had he wished it could have gone on indefinitely. But withdrawal was not enough for Augustine. "He had to live among men, for their benefit."[3] He emerged from solitude with the intention of bringing the gospel to both Christians and non-Christians.

Augustine's Influence

By the end of Augustine's life, his impact on non-Christians would prove astounding. Pagans, Donatists, Manicheans, Pelagians, and nominal Christians would receive the attention of most of his writings and sermons. He would "provoke the destruction of [these] old ways."[4] Through his ministry, "public paganism had been suppressed: the great temples were closed; the statues broken up, often by Christian mobs; the proud inscriptions that had proclaimed the unshakeable alliance of the ancient cities and their protecting gods, had been used to pave the public highway."[5] His writings would "demolish with quite exceptional intellectual savagery the whole of the ancient ethical tradition."[6] By his death, largely through his efforts, "the tide had turned away from Manicheanism among educated men."[7] B. B. Warfield claims he "not

2 *Nicene and Post-Nicene Fathers*, Series 1, Vol. 1, Philip Schaff, Ed. (Grand Rapids, MI: Christian Classics Ethereum Library), Ep. 94, 4.
3 Peter Brown, *Augustine of Hippo: A Biography*. Rev. ed. (Berkley, CA: University of California, 2000), 285.
4 Ibid, 270.
5 Ibid, 285.
6 Ibid, 326.
7 Ibid, 372.

merely created an epoch in the history of the Church, but has determined the course of its history in the West up to the present day."[8]

Augustine appears at the watershed of two worlds. Roman dominion was ending, and his native Africa was on the eve of destruction. It has been remarked that such "miserable existence of the Roman Empire in the West almost seems to have been prolonged for the express purpose of affording an opportunity for the influence of Augustine to be exerted on universal history."[9] Later we find figures as diverse as Luther, Freud, Aquinas, Anselm, Petrarch, Pascal, Kierkegaard, Nietzsche, and Wittgenstein drawn to his writings. The emperor Charlemagne slept with a copy of Augustine's *City of God* beneath his pillow. Descartes' Cartesianism was influenced by and in some places is a direct copy of Augustine's own epistemology. Augustine even anticipated certain aspects of modernism through his "romanticism," "self-assured subjectivity," and his "penetrating psychological insight."[10]

Amid such overwhelming influence the idea of Augustine the evangelist is often overlooked, but the thrust of his ministry portrays exactly that.[11] Among his first sermons were calls to repent and believe and to do so now, "while the world is still echoing to these words of mercy, before he comes to set up the tribunal of justice."[12] This statement is found in the introduction to the sermon, where Augustine urges his hearers to not make light of God's mercy and compassion, because God is also a God of truth and will judge the lost accordingly. The situation is urgent, he proclaims. His hearers must "renounce [sin]

---

8 B. B. Warfield, *Studies in Tertullian and Augustine*, 306.
9 Ibid, 310.
10 Charles Norris Cochrane, *Christianity and Classical Culture*, 417.
11 Thanks to Dr. Paul Sanchez's paper for pointing to the following sermon, along with apropos comments. "A Zealous Evangelist: Augustine's Urgent Call for Faith and Repentance" (unpublished paper), Oct. 29, 2015.
12 Sermon 94A.1, *The Works of Augustine: A Translation for the 21st Century*. III/1–11 (Hyde Park, NY: New City Press, 1990–1997), 87-94.

and be converted."[13] The only hope his hearers have is to "believe in the living God" and renounce "dead works." Augustine reminds them no one can attain salvation through good works, which is why they must have faith to be saved. "It's not, indeed, the merit of good works that brought you to faith; but faith begins, so that good works may follow… But can you believe God unless you have first renounced the devil? Therefore, in order to renounce him, repent; in order to be saved, believe."[14] At the close of this sermon Augustine answers the person who might ask, "What are we to do [to be saved]?" Repent, he exclaims. "Repent and you will be renewed."[15] In other sermons we find him wooing and warning his congregation: "I shall continue to call back the wandering; I shall seek out the lost."[16]

It would be impossible to overstate how influential Augustine was in rooting up entire systems of non-Christian thought and practices, while at the same time helping nominal Christians return to their first love or realize they had never had it to begin with. He was the epitome of a pastor who did the work of an evangelist. Without such a realization of Augustine, our view of him will be incomplete.

Life as a Bishop

Also, we should not think Augustine's life as a bishop was easy, nor should we assume Augustine was some type of super-apostle endowed with capabilities the rest of us don't have. This is not to say Augustine did not have a once-in-a-generation type of intellect, because he did. He was also self-disciplined and driven to a sensational degree. However, it is easy to lionize a man like Augustine to the extent of forget-

---

13 Ibid, 94A.2.
14 Ibid.
15 Ibid, 94A.9.
16 Ibid, 46.14.

ting he would make many mistakes. He would teach many erroneous doctrines. And he suffered from the same problem all ministers suffer from—a lack of time. He spent his mornings overseeing the church courts much like a judge. On other occasions he would appear in civil courts to ask for clemency for certain criminals. He would baptize, counsel, bury the dead, and officiate at people's marriages. He would train future ministers at his monastery which served as a seminary. He had free time for his own projects only in the evening, and even that was often taken up by ministry.

He gives us a glimpse of the demands of his ministry in a letter written to Possidius, his future biographer: "I am annoyed because of the demands which are thrust on me to write, arriving unannounced from here, there, and everywhere. They interrupt and hold up all the other things we have so neatly lined up in order. They never seem to stop and can't be put aside."[17] When we look closer at what kind of writing demands were being forced upon Augustine, we discover they are apologetic in nature. They include questions from skeptics on "the origin of the soul," treatises against the Arians, and another against a man who "said very many false and absurd things as well as things against the Catholic faith."[18] Augustine's desire was to return to his own writings, but he puts aside his personal work for the sake of spreading and defending the gospel amongst the lost. He once wrote to a heathen official: "When I obtain a little leisure from the urgent necessary business of those men who so press me into their service that I am neither able to escape them nor at liberty to neglect them, there are always subjects to which I must in dictating my amanuenses give the first place, because they are so connected with the present hour as

---

17 Letter 23A.3-4 (Divjak).
18 For the context of how the word "Catholic" is used in Augustine's writings, see chapter 3. It certainly does not mean "Roman" Catholic.

not to admit of being postponed."[19] He considered the call to ministry "an office of labor, and not of honor."[20] This is not to say he didn't enjoy his calling—he was especially fond of preaching, as we will see. But it is to say his understanding of ministry was realistic, not romantic, and yet he would persevere in it until the end of his life.

What is astonishing is that Augustine still made time to engage the lost. As a bishop he was intimately involved in the life of his congregation, as well as training others for the ministry. But whether it was through his sermons, epistles, or books, Augustine was concerned with seeing people saved. The task was not put on the backburner. It was not delegated to someone else. Like all ministers, Augustine's time was chewed up by various demands, many of them tedious. But Augustine never saw it as an excuse to neglect Paul's charge to Timothy to "do the work of an evangelist" (2 Tim. 4:5). This will be an important factor to remember as we look at the evangelism of Augustine. It was set against the backdrop of an intensely engaging and time-consuming pastoral ministry.

Setting of Augustine's Evangelism

Augustine's religious context was very much like our own. He did not live in a Christian world, even in the heyday of the Roman Empire's "Christianization." Christianity at best occupied a modest place compared to all the other spiritual options available at the time. Non-Christian groups were alive and well. Cults such as Manicheanism and Arianism were zealous missionaries. The pagan mystery cults of Augustine's day are the parents of certain New Age beliefs in the twenty-first century. The gods of the Graeco-Roman pantheon were

---

19 Letter 139.3.
20 *City of God*, 19.19; Letter 48.1.

still very much in vogue. Paganism had by no means given way to Christianity in the cities of Roman North Africa.[21] Augustine's day was one in which, when it came to religions and morals, "everyone did what was right in their own eyes." The climate required constant engagement with enemies both spiritual and physical.

Physically, he would survive assassination attempts on his life: "It once happened that I took a wrong turn at a crossroads and thus did not pass by a certain place where an armed band of Donatists lay in wait for me, expecting me to come."[22] The Donatists, his first foe, have been described as a type of religious terrorist group that had no qualms about killing their opponents—with Augustine being one of their chief targets. "They committed suicide by throwing themselves over cliffs, they devastated peaceful villages by sudden attacks, they murdered or demanded death for themselves indifferently."[23] Also, his territory would be invaded by Vandals. Rome would be destroyed by the Visigoths. The whole Mediterranean was a place constantly on the edge of starvation.[24] Hippo itself was a port for slaves and other nefarious practices. On one occasion Augustine's congregation liberated 120 slaves from a ship in Hippo's harbor. Although Augustine wasn't present at the time, the opportunity arose because of Augustine's reputation for what he calls "missions of mercy of this kind."[25]

Augustine was placed in "the unexpected backdrop of a robustly secular world, that had by no means rallied in its entirety to the values of the Christian church."[26] Historian Ramsay MacMullen observes the Roman Empire to have been predominantly non-Christian, especially

---

21 Brown, *Augustine of Hippo*, 447.
22 Enchiridion 5.17 (CCL 46:47); trans. Peebles, FOTC 2:382.
23 Frederick W. Dillstone, "The Anti-Donatist Writings," *Companion to Study of St. Augustine* (Oxford Press, 1955), 179.
24 Peter Brown, *The World of Late Antiquity* (New York, 1971), 12.
25 Letter (Divjak) 10.7.
26 Brown, *Augustine of Hippo*, 483.

in the earlier years of Augustine's ministry.[27] It was ripe for evangelism, and Augustine was the man for the hour. He "lived in a world that expected a man to stand up for his ideas, with tenacity and a certain sharpness,"[28] which is why at times he will deploy sarcasm, sometimes quite caustically, which would prove to be one of Augustine's most formidable weapons.[29] At times he seems "punch-drunk with cheap journalism." He could be rude when dealing with more serious opponents.[30] On one occasion in 399 A.D., Christians destroyed a statue of Hercules in a town near Augustine's Hippo. The pagans responded by killing sixty Christians. The town council wrote to Augustine demanding that the statue of Hercules be paid for by the Christians. Augustine responded: "If you say that Hercules is your god, we can take up a collection from everybody and buy you a god from the stonecutter. You, on the other hand, need to give us back the lives which your fierce hand wrested from us, and your Hercules will be restored to you exactly as the lives of so many are given back by you."[31] In other words, in the same way the Christians now dead will not be given back, neither will the statue of Hercules.

These are aspects of Augustine's methodology that will seem disturbing to modern tastes, but it can't be said he was not deeply invested in the lives of lost men, persuading them, pleading with them to come to the true faith. These were the days of heretics such as Pelagius, Nestorius and the just as formidable though more mysterious followers of Mani and Plotinus.[32] Augustine was always in the thick of it. Even among his own congregation, far from being cut off from the

---

27 Ramsay MacMullen, *Christianizing the Roman Empire* (New Haven, CT: Yale University, 1984), 83.
28 Brown, *Augustine of Hippo*, 492-493.
29 Ibid, 308.
30 Ibid, 270.
31 Letter 50, "To the city elders of Sufes."
32 Each individual is described in later chapters.

secular world, pagan gods were almost impossible to banish.[33] Both Augustine and his spiritual mentor Ambrose had to deal with people dancing wildly during worship, which they rebuked for being pagan.[34] It was a world influenced by astrologers, by soothsayers and by amulets, even in the church.[35]

No Longer the Recluse

This is the scene into which Augustine entered when he left the comforts of monastic security. Perhaps better put, it was this scene which pulled him out of such a retreat, into the clash and bustle of evangelistic opportunity. Even before he left this retreat, his desire was to see the lost saved. He would write long letters to former friends, eager to see them converted. His first treatise was *Against the Skeptics* and he wrote other early works against the Manicheans. Possidius speaks of a man of good fame and learning who "earnestly sought to see [Augustine], declaring that he was ready to reject all the passions and allurements of this world if he were but counted worthy to hear the Word of God from his lips. When this was brought to Augustine by trustworthy report, he longed to rescue that soul from the dangers of this life and from eternal death. So of his own accord he went in haste to that famous city and when he had seen the man he spoke to him frequently and exhorted him that in so far as God had blessed him he should pay to God what he had vowed."[36] Possidius describes Augustine as "longing" to rescue his soul and as going "in haste" to where he is. This will be a hallmark of Augustine throughout his life. When it comes to the lost, he is a man who craves their conversion. He is a man who goes

---

33 Brown, *Augustine of Hippo*, 243.
34 MacMullen, *Christianizing the Roman Empire*, 74. See also Augustine, sermon 311.5.
35 Brown, *Augustine of Hiipo*, 244.
36 Possidius, *Life of St. Augustine*, Ch. 3.

about it with hunger.

Augustine was called to ministry when he pursued a friend to Hippo in order to evangelize him: "I came to this city to see a friend, whom I thought I might gain for God."[37] When Augustine attended a sermon during this trip, the preacher spoke of the urgent needs of the church. As was common in the Roman Empire, the congregation realized Augustine was standing among them and began to shout for his ordination. Augustine states they grabbed him and pushed him forward to the preacher. Soon he would be made co-bishop of Hippo and one year later, bishop. Although Augustine would make it seem it was against his will, he never backs out. For the next forty years he would devote himself to the cause of the gospel. "The task to which he consciously gave himself was to apprehend, so far as it was given to him to apprehend, to proclaim, maintain, and defend the Catholic truth; and from this task he never swerved."[38] The world would never be the same because of it.

---

37 Sermon, 355.2.
38 B. B. Warfield, *Studies in Tertullian and Augustine,* 313.

two

Pre-conversion Influences on Augustine's Evangelism

Many factors contributed to molding Augustine into a missionary bishop. His study of Neoplatonism, Cicero, and the classics would play a dominant role in his work as a theologian. However, when it comes to his evangelism, there are three factors which interest us here.

Manicheanism - The Missionary Movement

At age 19 Augustine became a Manichean "Hearer." He followed this religion for nine years. He was able to participate in the rituals of Manicheanism while at the same time remaining indistinguishable from his environment—meaning he was able to keep his job as a professor of rhetoric while still identifying as a Manichee.[1] As a Hearer, he was also still allowed to live with his concubine. It was because of this status as a Manichean Hearer that Augustine was chosen by Symmachus for the chair of rhetoric in Milan, one of the most coveted

---

1 Brown, *Religion and Society in the Age of Saint Augustine* (London: Harper & Row, 1982), 109.

professional positions of the Roman Empire.[2]

The Manicheans were a type of Gnostic religious movement that had adopted some of the language of Christianity. They were influenced by Zoroastrianism and religions from ancient Babylon. They venerated the sun and moon and saw people as harboring a cosmic battle of the Kingdom of Light and the Kingdom of Darkness within themselves. They were radically dualistic as seen in their most important source of writings, written by Mani himself: "Two substances from the beginning of the world, the one light, the other darkness; the two are separated from each other."[3] These two "kingdoms" or substances are hostile to each other, and both have existed from eternity. Light is good and identified with spirit. Darkness is evil and is identified with matter. The conflict between the kingdom of darkness and the kingdom of light is what produces matter, which through a process of emanation extends to things like the earth, trees, grass and human bodies. They had their own body of writings which came to Mani through direct revelation. They used the Christian Scriptures as well, though viewing the Old Testament and certain portions in the New Testament as teaching a different—more monstrous—God than that which is found in the writings of Paul. In the early fourth century, Manicheanism shared a place with Christianity and Neoplatonism as one of the three great religions in the Roman Empire.[4]

The Manicheans were a "missionary religion."[5] Their founder, Mani (216 – 274 A.D.), thought of himself as a missionary. He borrowed the Pauline title of "Apostle of Jesus Christ" for his letters.[6] He was akin to a type of New Age guru in our own day, albeit with a bent on

---

2 Ibid.
3 From the *Fihrist* or "Catalogue."
4 See Stanley Romaine Hopper's "The Anti-Manichean Writings," in Companion to the Study of St. Augustine (Oxford: Oxford Press, 1955), 148.
5 Brown, *Religion and Society*, 94.
6 Ibid, 98.

evangelizing the world. Peter Brown says, "To study Manicheanism is to study the fate of a missionary religion in a world of shrinking horizons."[7] This particular mindset of the Manicheans would prove highly relevant for Augustine's future calling. This is what sets them apart from other groups in their day, even the Christians, since Christian outreach to people beyond their border had come to a disappointing halt in the time of Augustine. It was not so with Manicheanism, which had begun in the eastern provinces of Mesopotamia and within a hundred years had made headway in the western empire of Rome, as well as in the T'ang Empire of China.[8] They intended to supersede Christianity. They sought to create a world religion.[9]

Christianity and Manicheanism - Methodology Overlap

Despite grave doctrinal disparity between the two groups, we have here some commonalities as it pertains to how one was expected to respond to those outside the faith. Christianity at its root, like Manicheanism, is a missionary religion. The fact it was so influential in Rome only three hundred years after the crucifixion of Christ is proof of this. Like Paul and other early disciples, the Manichee teachers were obliged to travel.[10] The Manichee teachers would set out the seven great books of Mani in front of the Hearers, which would have included Augustine, and remind them "that 'the cry of salvation,' given forth in Babylon, had reached one's own town."[11] Manicheanism was constantly moving from the great cities into provincial towns and the safety of remote villages.[12] Manichean evangelism "involved engaging people in a dis-

---

7 Ibid, 104.
8 Ibid, 94-95.
9 Ironically, it would be Augustine who in large part kept it from happening.
10 Brown, *Religion and Society*, 111.
11 Ibid, 112.
12 Ibid, 113.

pute in intimate settings and winning them over."[13] Notably, Augustine himself "was won over [to the Manicheans] this way and actively worked, successfully, to win others."[14] Many of Augustine's friends would come to share his Manichee beliefs.

It is clear Augustine had imbibed some of this missionary outlook of the Manicheans. This is difficult to assess, of course, since a close reading of Scripture would produce a similar result with or without Manichean influence. It is perhaps more proper to suggest Manicheanism's missionary thrust was due to the Apostle Paul's influence on them and the general message of the gospel—that it is to be shared and spread. For this reason, it would be too much to suggest the Manicheans played a bigger role in Augustine's missionary methodology than the Scriptures. Yet, it is not too much to suggest the Manicheans, more so than the Christians of Augustine's day, were living out the missionary spirit found in the Scriptures, albeit with a grossly heretical doctrine. On a missionary level it was not a great leap for Augustine to have this same mentality when he became a Christian bishop, since such a missionary outlook was integral to the goal of both belief systems.

Turning the Tables on the Manicheans

Upon his conversion to Christianity, Augustine would dedicate one-third of his literary output to the refutation of the Manichean teachings.[15] Some claim Augustine's *Confessions* is, among other things, an evangelistic treatise against the Manicheans. Throughout Augustine's life, as a bishop, we find him encountering Manicheans with the gospel.

---

13 Horace E. Six-Means, *Augustine and Catholic Christianization* (New York: Peter Lang Publishing, 2011), 44.

14 Ibid.

15 J. A. Van Den Berg, *Biblical Argument in Manichean Missionary Practice* (Leiden: Koninklijke Brill NV, 2010), 1.

For instance, Augustine often takes the spirit of Manichean missions and applies it in a biblical way—to his old colleagues. One example of this is in religious debate. On several occasions, Augustine is found debating theological opponents in public bath houses. This would include the Manicheans. But it was the Manicheans who used public debate as a means of propagating their ideas.[16] Augustine simply takes it and uses it for the purpose of spreading the Christian message. For example, around 396 A.D. he wrote to the Donatist bishop in Hippo challenging him to a public debate for the purpose of letting the people see who had the truth: "Let us work at the business of their salvation and of our own. We are daily greeted by people with suppliant heads, begging us to settle their quarrels, but the disgraceful and dangerous division between our congregations is not a question of gold or silver, or of land and flocks. It is a dispute about our very head."[17]

On another occasion a Manichean teacher named Fortunatas was sought out for such a debate but having known Augustine when Augustine was still a Manichean, "he was afraid to meet him."[18] This is little wonder. Augustine was known to be a terror for demolishing opponents in public debate.[19] The social pressure became too much for Fortunatas and according to Augustine's friend Possidius, "he was greatly urged and shamed by the insistency of his followers and promised that he would meet him face to face and enter the contest of debate. So they met at an appointed time and place, where many who were interested and crowds of the curious quickly gathered. When the reporters' books had been opened, the discussion was begun on the first day and ended on the second."[20] Possidius relates that "the Manichaean

---

16 Brown, *Religion and Society*, 265.
17 Letter 33.5.
18 Possidius, *Life of St. Augustine*, Ch. 6.
19 Chadwick, *Augustine: A Very Short Introduction*, 20.
20 Possidius, *Life of St. Augustine*, Ch. 6.

teacher, as the evidence of the record proves, could neither refute the Catholic argument, nor could he prove that the sect of the Manichaeans was founded on truth." Because of the debate he lost his reputation among the Manicheans in Hippo. "Overwhelmed with confusion, he left the city of Hippo soon after and returned to it no more."

One time Augustine discovered "a certain Victorinus, a subdeacon of Malliana, is a Manichean, and that he hides his sacrilegious error under the name of cleric." Augustine goes on to say that the "subdeacon, posing as a Catholic, not only believed those intolerable blasphemies as the Manicheans do, but he taught them as vigorously as he could. He was discovered by his teaching when he trusted himself, so to speak, to his pupils."[21] We see here that followers of Mani often remained hidden under the shadow of the Catholic Church, so that "the problem of identifying the Manichee and of absorbing the convert devolved on the Catholic clergy."[22] This is one reason why Augustine's position as bishop is so influential when it comes to evangelism. He would be preaching to Manicheans on any given Lord's Day. As we will see, Augustine himself was a Manichean and then a Neoplatonist when first entering the church in Milan to hear the preaching of Ambrose—an influential step in his conversion to Christianity.

A Manichee merchant named Firmus will be converted after Augustine diverted from his sermon and began speaking on the cult of the Manicheans. [23] Firmus had been in the congregation and came to Augustine days later. He "fell down on his knees and prostrated himself at his feet, shedding tears and asking that the priest and his holy companions intercede with the Lord for his sins. For he confessed that he had followed the sect of the Manichaeans, had lived in it for

---

21 Letter 236.1-3.
22 Brown, *Religion and Society*, 110-111.
23 Ibid, 115.

many years and so had paid out much money in vain to the Manichaeans…But recently by the mercy of God he had been in the church and was converted and made a Catholic by Augustine's sermons."[24] Possidius describes their "wonder and marvel at the profound plan of God for the salvation of souls." In a declaration worthy of Augustine himself, Possidius exclaims, "We glorified and blessed His holy Name; for when He wishes and by whom He wishes and in whatever way He wishes, by those who know and those who do not know, He works the salvation of souls."[25]

Firmus would go on to become a Christian minister. He would "continue to satiate his zeal and his wanderlust by travelling from Bethlehem, to Sicily, to Africa, to Rome, to Ravenna," for the purpose of distributing Augustine's books and letters.[26] As a result, two former Manicheans teamed up to spread the Christian message throughout the Roman Empire. In this they emulated the early disciples and, though with a false message, the contemporary Manicheans. A Manichee teacher named Felix was converted when "Augustine argued in public in the church at Hippo while the people were present and the reporters took down the record. After the second or third meeting the emptiness and error of the sect were exposed and that Manichaean was converted to our faith and Church, as these writings will show if they are consulted."[27] Prior to Augustine's call to be a bishop, he wrote a book called *On the Advantages of Believing* "to a friend of mine who had been deceived by the Manicheans," showing once more how invested he was in delivering people from their errors. [28] He ended this book by explaining, "I only wanted to rescue you."[29]

---

24 Possidius, *Life of St. Augustine*, Ch. 15.
25 Ibid.
26 Brown, *Religion and Society*, 115.
27 Possidius, *Life of St. Augustine*, ch. 16.
28 *Revisions*, 1.14.1.
29 *On the Advantages of Believing*, 18.36.

B.B. Warfield notes Augustine, prior to his conversion, "was a man who had already lived through many experiences and had gathered much spoil in the process."[30] Warfield is alluding here to Augustine's time as a Manichee and Neo-Platonist. "He had sounded the depths of heresy in its most attractive form and had drunk the waters of philosophy in its culminating development; life in the conventicles of the sects and in the circle of cultured heathenism was alike familiar to him."[31] This would help Augustine to become the most formidable opponent of false religions in North Africa, if not the entire Roman Empire. He had once been one of them. He knew their doctrine. He knew their lingo. He knew their weaknesses. But he also knew their strengths, and knowing them, he would appropriate them for the sake of spreading the Christian gospel. "Augustine was successful against the Manicheans beginning in the 390s for two reasons. First, Augustine turned the Manichee tactic against them. He went on the offensive in proposing perplexing questions that highlighted the inconsistency of their positions. Second, he had the public debates recorded and published."[32] Augustine says the Manicheans had "two tricks for catching the unwary." They would find fault with the Scriptures and exaggerate their seemingly contradictory nature, and they would claim that Manicheanism was morally superior to other religions. This will become Augustine's greatest strategy against both the Manicheans and the pagans. He will demonstrate the inconsistency of the texts and history of each respective religion, and then do the same against their claim to moral superiority. He will then demonstrate the reliability and historical integrity of both the Scriptures and the Christian faith, while also showing that only Christianity can provide a basis for con-

---

30 B. B. Warfield, *Studies in Tertullian and Augustine*, 311.
31 Ibid.
32 Six-Means, *Augustine and Catholic Christianization*, 88.

sistent morality.

Ambrose - The Missionary Bishop

The second influence on Augustine's missionary methodology was Ambrose. Brown describes Ambrose as the great missionary bishop.[33] His sermons to his congregation "to pass through the drastic rite of baptism," which was linked at this time to conversion itself, were his most eloquent appeals.[34] The "great missionary bishop" was concerned with seeing people converted. Ramsay MacMullen describes Ambrose as a preacher who especially addressed non-Christians, "either to explain and recommend points to them, or to discredit their own beliefs."[35]

Brown theorizes that "without this strain in him, Ambrose would not have converted Augustine."[36] It was "the stirring rhetoric of Bishop Ambrose" that first drew Augustine into the Milan cathedral, as it would soon be Augustine's stirring rhetoric that would leave a spellbinding influence on his hearers in North Africa. In Book 5 of the *Confessions*, Augustine writes: "And so I came to Milan to Ambrose the bishop, known throughout the world as the best of men, devout in your worship...I was led to him by you, unaware that through him, I might be led to you." Elsewhere Augustine brags about Ambrose, "I was delighted by the sweetness of the language...This man taught the soundest way of salvation."[37] In Book 6 Augustine comments, "I did indeed hear him rightly preaching the word of truth to the people every Sunday, and I grow more and more certain that all the knots of

---

33 Brown, *Religion and Society*, 201.
34 Ibid.
35 Ramsay MacMullen, *Christianizing the Roman Empire* (New Haven, CT: Yale University, 1984), 64.
36 Brown, *Religion and Society*, 201.
37 *Confessions*, 5.13.23.

deceitful calumny, which those deceivers of ours had tied around the divine books, could be undone."[38] This last sentence is crucial. Not only was Ambrose used to convert the fledgling Augustine, but it was also Ambrose who showed Augustine the power of biblical apologetics, at times even in the pulpit. Ambrose demonstrated the Bible was not only true, but that it could be defended against its critics.

Like Ambrose, we will see Augustine throughout his life appealing to people through his preaching. He will plead and reason with his hearers. No subject will be left untouched when it comes to convincing his congregation to turn to the Lord. He spoke about God's love, hell, the existential crisis of man, the transience of life. Even more than an evangelistic writer, Augustine seems to have excelled as an evangelistic preacher.[39] When preaching on Luke 17:20-27, "Just as it was in the days of Noah, so will it be in the days of the Son of Man," Augustine notes how people live their lives carelessly until God's wrath falls on them.[40] Augustine describes the Lord in this passage as turning "to those who wish to live securely in the region of no security, and scared the wits out of them."[41] Augustine goes on, "They were all enjoying, you see, a spurious and pernicious sense of security, amusing themselves with every secular pastime you could think of, until Noah entered the ark, and the flood found them stripped and without any resources. So, by saying these things again now, he scared the daylights out of every living soul."[42] The ark symbolically cries out, "Be converted to God."[43] The ark as a figure of the Church was a tradition going back to Cyprian, and Augustine employed it effectively. "We have time to

---

38 Ibid, 6.3.4.
39 See chapter 10 of this book for an extensive treatment of this topic.
40 See Dr. Paul Sanchez's paper, "A Zealous Evangelist: Augustine's Urgent Call for Faith and Repentance" (unpublished paper), Oct. 29, 2015.
41 Sermon 114B.1.
42 Ibid.
43 Ibid, 114B.

wake up; it is not yet the day of judgment, not yet the flood. Beams of wood that cannot rot are still being cut from the forest, the ark is still being built."[44] An opportunity to be saved still exists, but the situation is urgent—men and women must repent or be washed away in the flood of God's judgment. "Noah is still crying out, the structure itself is still crying out."[45]

Not stopping there, Augustine would often use a type of hypothetical question and answer with his hearers: "But I would like someone, any of you, to tell me very briefly why you don't change your evil ways and make them into good ones. What can you lose by it?"[46] God had showed mercy to Nineveh when the city repented. God would show the same mercy to any who turns back to Him. But just as the flood came in Noah's day and destroyed the unrepentant, so will God's judgment come to those living in Augustine's day. He reminds his hearers that history has proven the truthfulness of God's Word time and again. Why live as though the promise of judgment was not imminent? "Very few things remain to be fulfilled," he warns. They must expect God's wrath to be poured out upon the earth, as promised in the Scriptures. "Nobody is permitted to stay here, all who come into this life are forced by the turning wheel of time to pass on. There's no place for sluggards; walk, or you will be dragged along."[47] Temptation presses them to take the path of ease and pleasure, which most people travel, but "this road in the end leads to doom."[48] He urges them to choose the road to eternal life. Such sermons are typical of Augustine, but they are also reminiscent of Ambrose.[49]

Even Ambrose's call to ministry was like Augustine's own call de-

---

44 Ibid.
45 Ibid.
46 Ibid.
47 Ibid.
48 Ibid.
49 See Chapter 10 of this book for a fuller treatment of Augustine's evangelistic preaching.

cades later. Neither of them had been looking to be a minister when the crowd suddenly seizes upon them, compelling them to pastor their church. In Ambrose's case, he was a governor sent to Milan after the Archbishop died. Riots were breaking out among the people regarding who should be the next bishop. Ambrose encouraged them to act in an orderly manner when a little child cried out, "Let Ambrose be our bishop." The crowd joined in the cry. In a week Ambrose was baptized and placed into ministry. Augustine would have undoubtedly linked Ambrose's call to ministry with his own when he experienced something similar in Hippo.

Though never close, Ambrose and Augustine would remain friendly until Ambrose's death. Ambrose was Augustine's hero. Augustine even urged a Milanese deacon, Paulinus, to write a life of Ambrose.[50] Although the two saw themselves as pastors and shepherds of souls, they shared a similar relish for evangelistic preaching and a commitment to spreading and defending the gospel among the lost. Without Ambrose, there would have been no Augustine, much less Augustine the evangelist.

Augustine's Mother, Monica

A colossal though overlooked impact on Augustine's evangelism was his mother, Monica. Augustine lived and worked in a man's world. Growing up in North Africa, it would have been illegal for Augustine's mother to pass on her Christian faith, since the children were expected to follow the father's religion. But Augustine's mother took him to church while growing up and even enrolled him as a catechumen. She sang hymns to him and prayed over him. Augustine would later praise his mother for this along with her example of Christian living. Au-

---

50 Brown, *Augustine of Hippo*, 412.

gustine attributes his conversion to his mother's prayers, which is no trivial compliment: "And now thou [God] didst 'stretch forth thy hand from above' and didst draw up my soul out of that profound darkness [of Manicheism] because my mother, thy faithful one, wept to thee on my behalf more than mothers are accustomed to weep for the bodily deaths of their children…And thou didst hear her, O Lord, thou didst hear her and despised not her tears when, pouring down, they watered the earth under her eyes in every place where she prayed. Thou didst truly hear her."[51]

While Augustine was off playing the prodigal bohemian, his mother stayed on his trail, praying for him, urging him to consider the faith more deeply. Such an example and devotion didn't go unheeded by Augustine either, flee from it as he may, at least initially. "Nearly nine years passed in which I wallowed in the mud of that deep pit [of Manicheanism] and in the darkness of falsehood, striving often to rise, but being all the more heavily dashed down. But all that time this chaste, pious, and sober widow—such as thou dost love—was now more buoyed up with hope, though no less zealous in her weeping and mourning; and she did not cease to bewail my case before thee, in all the hours of her supplication."[52]

In many ways this is the epitome of the evangelistic spirit. Monica's object in life was the conversion of others, and in this case Augustine. The intransigence of a mother's love for her son is certainly part of the motive here, but the spiritual dynamism of her encounters with Augustine must chiefly be attributed to her zeal to see Augustine come to Christ. Perhaps more impressive is her refusal to compromise or wa-ter-down the truth for her lost son. One could imagine the temptation to lie to oneself about the state of an unconverted child, but Monica

---

51 *Confessions*, 3.11.19.
52 Ibid, 3.11.20.

never seems to do this. She knows her son is lost. She tells her son that he is lost. She tells God that her son is lost. But she persistently prays, shares her faith, and demonstrates the reality of that faith by her own life. Although not all parents are privy to seeing their children come to Christ before their death, Monica did. Shortly after Augustine's conversion, Monica died of a fever as they waited for a boat back to Africa. But according to Augustine she died content, knowing her son had been won for Christ.

It is another trait of Monica's which Augustine seems to have imbibed as an evangelist, however. Monica can be seen as overbearing at times. At one point in his life Augustine even sneaks away at night to keep her from following him to Rome. Had Monica known, she wouldn't have let him make the trip, but Augustine notes it was the overriding sovereignty of God that got him on board a ship and sent him across the Mediterranean Sea. She didn't realize it at the time, but God was going to bring him to the faith by doing so. "She did not know what joy thou wast preparing for her through my going away. Not knowing this secret end, she wept and mourned and saw in her agony the inheritance of Eve—seeking in sorrow what she had brought forth in sorrow. And yet, after accusing me of perfidy and cruelty, she still continued her intercessions for me."[53]

This should encourage parents to continue praying and to be hopeful for the conversion of their children even in the face of seemingly impossible situations. On the surface, Rome seemed like the last place in the world for a young upstart to be converted. It would be like an unbelieving child moving to join a liberal circle in New York City or San Francisco. Monica's hopes were dashed. But as Augustine tells us, she continued to pray and wait on the Lord, not knowing the Lord in

---

53 Ibid, 5.8.15.

is His sovereignty was going to use such a move to convert him.

Eventually she followed him to Milan, another trip north across the sea. Her tenacity is both alarming and admirable. She won't let her object go, in this case Augustine's conversion. Though hyper-obsessive at times, Monica demonstrates an encouraging energy which every Christian could use, especially when it comes to evangelism. She is dauntless. She has great faith in God, but she also knows she has a role to play as well. God uses means to convert people, and often those means are a person's mother—whether through prayer, sharing the gospel, demonstrating the faith in her own life, or usually all of the above. Monica is an example to parents everywhere to continue evangelizing their children even in the face of defeat or rejection.

This same feature will be seen in Augustine the evangelist throughout his life. As we have already seen, he often drops everything in pursuit of some friend who has drifted from the faith or perhaps has never believed. Whether through writing or by making a physical trip to the friend's location, Augustine goes after his man until the man is converted or intellectually defeated—and even then, Augustine is typically quick to keep encouraging his friend to turn to the Lord and showing him kindness until he does. Augustine seems to have had this trait even as a Manichean, but as a Christian he feels he finally has not only the true gospel, but one which can be argued for intellectually, as well.

It would be unhealthy to speculate too much on the genetic influence of Monica on Augustine, but the tenacity we find in Augustine—and that which made him such a successful evangelist—is certainly present in his mother. In Monica, Augustine was exposed to a genuine Christian who was eager to see her son come to the Lord. When Augustine was converted, he would have the same mentality until the day of his death, praying, writing, preaching, and pleading with the lost to come out of darkness and into the Lord's marvelous light.

Conclusion

Though many factors led to the making of Augustine the evangelist, it was especially important that he had spent time at the meat pots of Babylon, absorbing belief systems which he would go on to dismantle later in life. His experience also gave him a wide perspective of evangelism methodologies, some of them better than others—such as the zeal (without knowledge) of the Manicheans. It would be like someone in our day being converted out of the Church of the Latter-Day Saints or the Jehovah's Witnesses. While decrying the horrid doctrine of both groups and while acknowledging that their proselytizing fervor must be attributed at least in part to the works-based demand on them to do it—such a person would still learn certain approaches or tactics that he could carry over to his evangelism for the Christian faith. For instance, think of certain door-knocking experiences such a person would have. Much of evangelism is simply getting the courage and experience of doing it. The man who is converted out of these cults has already spent time proselytizing strangers and friends, despite wrong motives and a false gospel.

This is similar to what Augustine did when he was converted to Christianity. Nowhere is there found any compromise in Augustine when it comes to the Manichean system of thought. Rather, it is his ability to appropriate the tactics used by the Manicheans for the sake of Christianity that is so effective when he begins to evangelize his former group. It was also the experience he had gained while proselytizing others as a Manichean that helped him better understand what he was getting into whenever he became a Christian, at least when it came to certain basic elements of evangelizing: how to engage with strangers, how to write polemical tracts, how to debate.

When it comes to the actual life of the evangelist, however, it was Monica's influence which he seems to have unconsciously absorbed. Her evangelistic energy, prayers, tears and even obsession for the Lord's cause were seen in Augustine immediately upon his conversion. Without him knowing it, the Lord had been preparing him to do the work of the evangelist even before he'd been saved, showing him what such a spirit is like in the person of his mother. Ambrose would provide the finishing touch by demonstrating to Augustine what evangelistic preaching is and how a minister should go about rescuing the lost, especially from the pulpit. When such traits are combined to an intellect as behemoth as Augustine's, we can better understand why Augustine was sought out to be a bishop shortly after his conversion, and why he was so succesful.

That said, Augustine would be the first to pump the breaks on any kind of celebrating that made him out to be more than merely a man. He was deeply aware of his shortcomings and pride, which made him all the more effective as a minister. To have great intellectual and even evangelistic abilities are nothing if in the same man resides an inability to see his own weaknesses and lusts—if that same man is proud or thinks he is indispensable, for instance. This was perhaps Augustine's greatest strength: not his abilities, but his understanding of how weak he was apart from the grace of God. But because of this grace, Augustine realized he could have great confidence when ministering the gospel and evangelizing the lost, which brings us to the next chapter.

three

Optimistic Evangelism

Augustine's evangelism can aptly be described as optimistic, both in the beginning of his ministry and at the end, although in very different respects. In the beginning of his ministry, before the fall of Rome, his outlook is optimistic in a way very much resembling the modern concept of postmillennialism. Such an interpretation was growing in popularity at the time. Rome had been Christianized by Constantine fifty years before Augustine's conversion. Pagans were coming to the faith en masse. So were the aristocracy. Between the fourth and fifth centuries, the number of Christians in the Roman Empire had grown from five to thirty million.[1] It made sense "Eusebius, Ambrose, Prudentius, and Orosius…had predicted an era of unprecedented peace and prosperity under the auspices of Christianity and as a direct outcome of its emergence as a world religion uniting all men in the cult of the true God."[2] Virgil's "Sibylline prophecy" about a child coming

---

1 MacMullen, *Christianizing the Roman Empire*, 86.
2 Ernest L. Fortin, "St. Augustine," *History of Political Philosophy*, Levi Strauss, Ed. (Chicago: University of Chicago Press, 1987), 176-205.

into the world as the forerunner to some golden age was popularly interpreted as Jesus.[3] Seeing the dominance of Christianity across the Roman empire, it seemed natural it would keep expanding.

Augustine's Early "Postmillennialism"

Augustine is no exception to such a view. Early on in his ministry he thinks it inevitable the church will advance throughout the world. "The whole world is now Christ's chorus; from the east to the west, Christ's chorus echoes in harmony."[4] "All are astonished to see the entire human race converging on the Crucified, from emperors down to beggars in their rags…No age group is passed over, no lifestyle, no learned tradition…persons of every rank have already come, of every level of income and of every form of wealth. It is high time for all and sundry to be inside."[5] Elsewhere he boasts, "And first let him see the world itself to be changed, lately worshipping idols, now worshipping God…Already the Pagans that are left are in dread of the 'changed' state of things: and those who will not suffer themselves to be changed see the churches full; the temples deserted; see crowds here, and there solitude. They marvel at the things so changed; let them read that they were foretold; let them lend their ears to Him who promised it; let them believe Him who fulfills that promise."[6] The decline of paganism was demonstrated by temples becoming empty and even dismantled. Edicts were passed forbidding pagan sacrifice. Tribesmen outside of the Roman Empire were coming to Augustine and others to ask to be instructed in the Christian faith.[7] Churches generally were well attended.

---

3 Henry Chadwick, *Augustine of Hippo: A Life* (Oxford Press, 2009), 18.
4 Sermon on Psalm 149.7.
5 *Essential Sermons*, Ed. Daniel Doyle (New York, NY: New City Press, 2007), 362.
6 Augustine, Sermon 44.
7 Chadwick, *Augustine of Hippo: A Life*, 71.

Such optimism was surprising for many in Augustine's congregation. Many Christians despised paganism and perhaps even avoided pagan rituals that would contaminate them, "but they did not expect to live in a society where paganism had been swallowed up entirely… The idea of a total Catholic society had remained beyond their horizon of the possible."[8] But in 404 A.D., a few years before the fall of Rome, Augustine envisioned Christianity as a "truly universal religion."[9] He "dared to think the unthinkable thought that Christianity could be the faith of an entire society."[10] Augustine believed "the Catholic Church, now 'fully grown up,' was destined to absorb all other faiths."[11] "The church's expansion was foreordained."[12] He asked, "Who shall remove the preordained course (the *praedestinatio*) of God?"[13] When preaching to a congregation interspersed with pagan notables, Augustine tried persuading them to the faith by pointing out that "the whole world raises a shout," a reference to the influx of pagans coming into the church.[14]

Augustine's time in Rome and Milan helped contribute to his early optimism. "He encountered a cosmopolitan Church, wielding influence over emperors and officials, occupying a place of leadership in society, confident of its power to absorb, mould and transform it."[15] Such a church was "assured of its mission, confident of conquering a world which had been promised to it by the prophecies of the Old Testament."[16] This is the original meaning of the word "Catholic." Far

8 Brown, *Augustine of Hippo*, 460.
9 Ibid, 461.
10 Ibid.
11 *Essential Sermons*, 187.
12 Brown, *Augustine of Hippo*, 216.
13 Sermon on Ps. 32.14.
14 *Essential Sermons*, 382.
15 R.A. Markus, *Saeculum: History and Society in the Theology of St. Augustine* (Cambridge: Cambridge University Press, 1970), 105-106.
16 Ibid, 113.

from being centralized in a particular location such as Rome, Augustine viewed the church as having a universal impact and presence in the world. More importantly, it consisted in agreement with churches around the world and communion with them.[17] Because Christ is King in all the nations of the world, "so is His Church made manifest, not in Africa alone…but spread abroad throughout the world."[18]

When he went to Africa, he encountered a very different type of church. Catholics "were an insecure minority" in Africa.[19] Donatism was the religion of the people, following the tradition of Tertullian, who saw the church as mutually exclusive from the world. They were separatists who had no desire to be unified with other churches. They taught that the church was confined only to the Donatists, and the Donatists were to be found mainly in North Africa. They considered everyone else to be compromisers.

Despite being the religious minority, Augustine's optimism never wavered. He was called upon to lead the church at Hippo in part because of his potential ability to advance and defend the Catholic position against the Donatist majority.[20] He believed the Donatist conception of the Church was too small. The Donatists felt they alone were heirs of the true Church, but such a view did not take seriously the power of God to disciple the nations or extend His church throughout the world. Arguing from Genesis 22:18, "In thy seed all the nations of the earth shall be blessed," Augustine criticizes the Donatists for not "holding communion with all the nations of the earth," unlike the Catholics, who saw the Church as universal and ever-expanding.[21] The Donatists were content to be isolated from the rest of the Christians,

---

17 Ibid.
18 Ibid.
19 Ibid, 111.
20 Chadwick, *Augustine: A Life*, 64.
21 Augustine, "Against the Letter of Petilianus," 1.23.

which flies in the face of the prophetic blessing given to Abraham that his seed would be a blessing to all people.[22] This being the case, how then could the Donatists claim to be a faithful church? Augustine's frustration with the Donatists' narrow outlook was rarely hidden: "The clouds of heaven proclaim the house of God being built over the whole earth; and the frogs croak from their pond: 'We only are the true Christians.'"[23] For Augustine, the Donatists couldn't claim to be the true church since they were content to be confined only to Africa. Rather, God's church "could be nothing other than the one Church spread over the earth."[24] Again, this is not Roman Catholicism. This is the power of the gospel making certain that the Church would be built across the earth. Through such advancement, there would be agreement in doctrine, practice, and communion among the churches, whether in Africa, Rome, Spain or elsewhere. This is not an appeal to a centralized authority in the church but rather to the universality of a shared belief and practice.[25]

Later, after the fall of Rome in 410, Augustine's optimism would be tempered but still apparent. He lost enthusiasm for the idea that the gospel would save most people, but he was unwavering in his conviction it would still save, still advance, and still build up the church. It would not bring about "a fully Christian society" but it would accomplish what God had set out to do—glorify His name through the advance of the church, despite the conflict and defeats God's people may suffer.[26]

The disasters of Rome at the hand of the Visigoths deflated any idea of a "Christian Era." Christians were now unpopular. Their lives were in jeopardy. Their faith was in peril. Augustine, always the evangelist,

---

22 Six-Means, *Augustine and Catholic Christianization*, 75.
23 Sermon on Psalm 95.11.
24 Markus, *Saeculum*, 113.
25 Chadwick, *Augustine of Hippo: A Life*, 56.
26 *City of God*, Tr. Marcus Dods (New York City: Random House, 1993), 2.19.

spoke at this time "to confused men, lingering in a hundred ways on the fringe of paganism, with pagan relatives, pagan neighbors, loyalties to their city that could only be expressed by pagan ceremonies."[27] It was a setback, but Augustine's optimism was tenacious. It was not the idea of Christian dominion over the whole world that inspired it, however.

The Millennium Is Now

The first reason for Augustine's sustained optimism is his view of the millennium. Augustine became convinced that millennial perfection could not be achieved in this world, although it would be achieved by the end of history. Likewise, humans had no idea when the end of the world would take place nor how it would happen. He no longer believed an earthly institution such as the Roman Empire could ever be pure or entirely Christianized. And yet, far from being pessimistic about the future, he began to see the millennium as having begun with the advent of Christ. Hence, the millennium was not something still to come. It was here, and the saints are now reigning with Christ: "the Church could not now be called His kingdom or the kingdom of heaven unless His saints were even now reigning with Him."[28] The battle had already been fought and Christ had conquered. Although Satan still had influence in this world, it had been vastly reduced. Eventually, even the little that he had would be taken from him.

Augustine's view of Satan and the millennium was not new at the time. In fact, oddly enough, the same view is found in the *Life of Antony*, written by Athanasius sometime between 356 – 362 A.D., when Augustine was a toddler. Antony had been a mystical Christian recluse. Born to wealth, he renounced it all as a teenager and went to

---

27 Brown, *Augustine of Hippo*, 312.
28 *City of God*, 20.9.

the desert to contemplate God and fight with the devil. Even before his death, Antony had gained a wide following among those who were increasingly annoyed by the carnal Christianity of the Roman Empire. People began to follow the example of Antony, leading to a large monastic movement.

The story of Antony's life played a significant role in the conversion of Augustine. Although Augustine had not read his story at the time he was converted, he tells us in his *Confessions* that a certain Ponticianus stopped by one day and began to relate to him about the desert monk's achievements: "He spoke of Antony, the Egyptian monk, whose name was in high repute among thy servants, although up to that time not familiar to me. When he learned this, he lingered on the topic, giving us an account of this eminent man, and marveling at our ignorance. We in turn were amazed to hear of thy wonderful works so fully manifested in recent times—almost our own."[29]

Ponticianus goes on to relate how he himself was converted to God upon hearing about Antony. He and three others had gone out for a walk close to the city walls one day. The group broke off into twos, and the other pair of friends "came upon a certain cottage where lived some of thy servants…where they found the book in which was written the life of Antony! One of them began to read it, to marvel and to be inflamed by it. While reading, he meditated on embracing just such a life, giving up his worldly employment to seek thee alone." The man then turned to his friend with "shame" and "anger," exclaiming: "Tell me, I beg you, what goal are we seeking in all these toils of ours? What is it that we desire? What is our motive in public service? Can our hopes in the court rise higher than to be 'friends of the emperor'?… But if I chose to become a friend of God, see, I can become one now."[30]

---

29 *Confessions*, 8.6.14.
30 Ibid.

This friend resolved then and there to pursue a life of godliness, and the other, shaken by such a revelation, decided "to share in so great a service for so great a prize."[31] Shortly after, the other two friends, which included Ponticianus, met up with them and told them it was time to head back. But the first two made known to Ponticianus their resolve to live for the Lord and warned them "not to take it ill if they refused to join themselves with them." Ponticianus and his companion congragulated the two friends on their decision and asked them to pray for them.

Augustine tells us that while Ponticianus was relating this story, Augustine realized "how ugly I was, and how crooked and sordid, bespotted and ulcerous."[32] He realized how empty his life was in contrast to those who had given their lives to the Lord. "Thus was I inwardly confused, and mightily confounded with a horrible shame, while Ponticianus went ahead speaking such things."[33] After Ponticianus left, Augustine seized his friend who was in the room with him and shouted: "What is the matter with us? What is this? What did you hear? The uninstructed start up and take heaven, and we—with all our learning but so little heart—we wallow in flesh and blood! Because others have gone before us, are we ashamed to follow, and not rather ashamed at our not following?"[34] This scene would end with "the voice of a boy or a girl I know not which—coming from the neighboring house, chanting over and over again, 'Pick it up, read it; pick it up, read it,'" which Augustine took as a divine command to open up the Bible and read the first passage he saw.[35] Famously, this led to his conversion.

Doubtless Augustine would become acquainted with Athanasius'

---

31 Ibid.
32 Ibid, 8.7.16.
33 Ibid.
34 Ibid, 8.8.19.
35 Ibid, 8.12.29.

biography of Antony soon after his conversion. The story had been the catalyst for his new birth in Christ and it would also help shape his understanding of Satan and his limited control on earth. In the midst of his duels with Satan, Antony gives commentary on this theme of Satan's limits: "'Since the Lord made his sojourn with us, the enemy is fallen and his powers have diminished. For this reason, though he is able to do nothing, nevertheless like a tyrant fallen from power, he does not remain quiet but issues threats...They know that as we advance, they are weekend. Indeed, if they had authority, they would not permit one of us Christians to live.'"[36]

When speaking of Job, Antony rhetorically asks why Satan, if powerless, was able to afflict Job with such maladies as death to his children and disease to his flesh? Antony exclaims, "It was God who turned over the testing of Job to him. It is clear that because he was capable of doing nothing, he asked this...If he possessed strength, he would not have made the request."[37] In fact, the devil does not have authority even over pigs, since the demons must ask Christ's permission before entering them.

Augustine's optimism is reminiscent of Antony's own, who boasts the demons complain that "'there are Christians everywhere, and even the desert has filled with monks.'"[38] Antony responds, "Christ in his coming reduced you to weakness, and after throwing you down he left you defenseless."[39] Antony goes on to encourage Christians to treat the demons "'with utter contempt...And let us consider in our soul that the Lord is with us, he who routed them and reduced them to idleness. Let us likewise always understand and take it to heart that while the

---

36 Athanasius, *The Life of Antony and the Letter to Marcellinus*, Tr. Robert C. Gregg (Mahwah, NJ: Paulist Press, 1980), 51-52.
37 Ibid, 52.
38 Ibid, 62.
39 Ibid.

Lord is with us, the enemies will do nothing to us.'"[40]

Augustine's view did not arise out of a vacuum. This was an interpretation of Scripture that appears in one of the most popular books of the time. However, what was new was Augustine's ability to apply such a view to specific events such as the fall of Rome and the persecutions against God's people. No longer seen as an apocalyptic blow, it is now regarded as unsurprising. The City of God and the City of the World are forced to coexist. Events such as the fall of Rome will inevitably take place. The spread of the Church is not dependent on the Roman Empire or any other worldly institution. The Church is a "kingdom militant, in which conflict with the enemy is still maintained, and war carried on with warring lusts, or government laid upon them as they yield, until we come to that most peaceful kingdom in which we shall reign without an enemy."[41] This idea parallels what he says in an earlier sermon: "Then let the Church go forth, let her march ahead; the road is prepared, our highway has been prepared by our Commander in chief. Let us be zealous in treading the paths of good works, for that is our manner of marching."[42] Christ's advent has guaranteed the eventual and total destruction of the City of the World at the eschaton, but until that time, we are in a spiritual war.

Such a view is still very much in keeping with a postmillennial view of history, although a strict application would be anachronistic. Augustine is not a postmillennialist. His optimism, however, is similar to what would later be called postmillennialism, even after the fall of Rome. Others have claimed he is an amillenialist.[43] Regardless of whether he can be squeezed into more modern categories of the end times debate, Augustine clearly believes history "would be marked by

40 Ibid, 62-63.
41 *City of God*, 20.9.
42 Sermon on Psalm 32, 2:10.
43 See Kim Riddlebarger's *A Case for Amillenialism*, 40.

the ever-increasing influence of the church in overturning evil in the world before the Lord's return."[44]

In *City of God*, written after the fall of Rome, Augustine comments on Nahum 1:14 and 2:1: "We already see the graven and molten images, that is, the idols of the false gods, exterminated through the gospel, and given up to oblivion as of the grave, and we know that this prophecy is fulfilled in this very thing."[45] He predicts that "even those nations which are not under the Roman authority, being suddenly terrified by the news of Thy wonderful works, shall become a Christian people."[46] He says about Haggai 2:6, "'Thus saith the Lord of hosts, Yet one little while, and I will shake the heaven, and the earth, and the sea, and the dry land; and I will move all nations, and the desired of all nations shall come.' The fulfillment of this prophecy is in part already seen, and in part hoped for in the end...So we see all nations moved to the faith; and the fulfillment of what follows, "And the desired of all nations shall come," is looked for at His last coming. For before men can desire and wait for Him, they must believe and love Him."[47]

There was a second reason for Augustine's optimism, however—his increasing awareness of God's providence and predestination in the conversion of sinners. Far from stifling Augustine's evangelism, it was the only thing that sustained it during the tougher years of his ministry.

---

44 Zoba, "Future Tense," Christianity Today (October 2, 1995), 20.
45 *City of God*, 18.31.
46 Ibid, 18.32.
47 Ibid, 18.35.

four

Predestination and Evangelism

Augustine's opponents never did show the optimism of Augustine, lacking as they did any such doctrine as predestination. The Donatists, for instance, felt that "the unworthiness of some of its members" had jeopardized any sense that the church would inevitably expand or even persist.[1] Their sectarianism amongst themselves and others ensured an eventual demise.

The Pelagians would have worse problems. If men had libertarian freedom and if it were possible to lose your salvation, what guarantee is there that anyone will choose to become Christians? And, once converted, what guarantee is there that anyone will stay Christian? What certainty is there that the church will continue to exist through the ages? Unlike Augustine, such groups couldn't be certain Christ and His Church should have "the uttermost parts of the earth as Thy possession" (Ps. 2:8). They could not even be certain that anyone would be saved.

---

1 Brown, *Augustine of Hippo*, 311.

Pelagius and Pelagianism - The Novel Doctrine

Pelagianism gained traction in the later part of Augustine's life. Pelagius was a British monk who resided in Rome and became popular as a spiritual counsellor for the wealthy. The Pelagian system was built upon the assumption, in his own words, "that man is able to be without sin, and that he is able to keep the commandments of God."[2] When it came to salvation man did not need divine grace in the sense of an inward help. Man did not inherit sin or any taint of sin from Adam. The bad example of Adam and the power of habit are responsible for influencing man to act in sinful ways, but man is born good, without sin. "Nothing makes well-doing so hard as the long custom of sins which begins from childhood and gradually brings us more and more under its power until it seems to have in some degree the force of nature."[3] Hence, salvation was ultimately up to man. He needed no divine interference for making it happen.

Augustine, followed by others, pointed out that such a doctrine was unknown among Christianity until Pelagius invented it in the fifth century. B. B. Warfield remarks "this was not only new in Christianity; it was even anti-Christian."[4] Jerome spoke of Pelagianism as "the heresy of Pythagoras and Zeno."[5] Others since have identified the Pelagian concept of freedom with that of paganism.[6] Many have noted it resonates more with Cicero's words than anything like the Apostle Paul or even Jesus: "For gold, lands, and all the blessings of life, we have to return thanks to the Gods; but no one ever returned

---

2 Pelagius, *On Nature and Grace*, 49.
3 Letter, Pelagius to Demetrias.
4 Warfield, "The Origen and Nature of Pelagianism," 12.
5 Preface to Book iv. of his work on Jeremiah.
6 B. B. Warfield cites Dr. DePressensé's *Trois Prem. Siécles*, ii. 375 as an example.

thanks to the Gods for virtues."[7] According to Pelagianism, virtue is something attained by man without the direct aid of God. Because of this, Warfield notes "the real question at issue was whether there was any need for Christianity at all; whether by his own power man might not attain eternal felicity; whether the function of Christianity was to save, or only to render an eternity of happiness more easily attainable by man."[8]

One of Augustine's achievements against the Pelagians was to demonstrate that their view of human nature was based upon an inadequate view of the complexity of human motivation.[9] Augustine taught that human action was the "culmination of an inner evolution" of different thoughts, emotions, circumstances and the like, all of which were bent towards evil in the unconverted man. In fact, even if evil men chose to do the ostensibly good thing, their motives for acting could not be good since their nature made it impossible. "Men choose because they love," but evil men can only love evil, not the good.[10] Augustine would write, "From a depth that we do not see, comes everything that you can see." Elsewhere he explains, "We have established…that what each man chooses to pursue and to love lies in his own will."[11] Unbelievers don't choose to act from a motive of loving God and loving their neighbor. They choose to act from self-seeking motives—since that is what an unbeliever's nature demands.[12] Paul hints at this in his letter to Titus, saying "to the defiled and unbelieving, nothing is pure; but both their minds and their consciences are defiled" (Tit. 1:15-16).

Speaking on original sin, Augustine comments, "the sin which these [Adam and Eve] committed was so great that it impaired all

---

7 *History of the Councils of the Church* (E.T.), ii. 446, note 3.
8 Warfield, "The Origen and Nature of Pelagianism," 13.
9 Brown, *Augustine of Hippo*, 373.
10 Ibid, 375.
11 *Free Choice*, 1.16.114.
12 Sermon, 165, 3.

human nature—in this sense: that the nature has been transmitted to posterity with a propensity to sin and a necessity to die. Moreover, the kingdom of death so dominated mankind that all would have been hurled, by a just punishment, into a second and endless death had not some been saved from this by the gratuitous grace of God."[13] In another place he announces, "Every individual springs from a condemned stock and, because of Adam, must be first evil and carnal, only later to become good and spiritual by the process of rebirth in Christ."[14] Such a view comports with Scripture, which states that "surely I was sinful at birth" (Ps. 51:5 NIV) and "the wicked are estranged from the womb: they go astray as soon as they be born, speaking lies" (Ps. 58:3). God tells Noah "the imagination of man's heart is evil from his youth" (Gen. 8:21). Augustine points out it is not God's fault, however, since such sin was contracted from Adam's rebellion against God in the garden: "But the flaw which darkens and weakens all those natural goods, it has not contracted from its blameless Creator…but from that original sin, which it committed of its own free-will."[15]

Freedom and the Will

Towards the end of Augustine's life he wrote a book called *Revisions*, which contained retractions and explanations of things he wrote earlier in his ministry. Much of this book focuses on Augustine's view of the will. Early on, while considering where evil comes from, he emphasized the freedom of man's actions and the justice of God for condemning such actions. Later the Pelagians picked up on these earlier writings and used them to claim Augustine "had taken up their cause" as a young man, only to change his views. In the *Revisions*, Au-

---

13 *City of God*, 14.1.
14 Ibid, 15.1.
15 *On Nature and Grace*, 54, 55, 59.

gustine explains himself: "Because God's grace, which was not an issue at the time, was not mentioned in these and similar words of mine, the Pelagians think, or could think, that we held their opinion. But in vain do they think this…The will itself, then, cannot be an upright and virtuous source of life for mortal men unless it is freed by God's grace from the slavery whereby it has become a slave of sin, and is helped to overcome its vices."[16]

Notice Augustine is not denying freedom of the will. Man is free to act, but only in accordance with his nature. An evil nature desires that which is evil, and thus can only choose evil. Augustine says, "There is…always within us a free will—but it is not always good."[17] In several places the Scriptures speak of unbelieving man as being enslaved to evil. Jesus says, "Everyone who commits sin is a slave to sin" (Jn. 8:34). Paul speaks of this same concept in at least four of his letters, perhaps best summarized by his statement to Titus: "For we ourselves were once foolish, disobedient, led astray, slaves to various passions and pleasures" (Tit. 3:3a; see also Gal. 4:8-9; Rom. 6:6-20, 7:14; 2 Tim. 2:25-26). Jeremiah asks, "Can the Ethiopian change his skin or the leopard its spots? Then may you also do good who are accustomed to do evil" (Jer. 13:23). A leopard can't stop being a leopard. A snake can't cease to act like a snake. The very nature of the creature demands it. So it is with the lost person. A bad tree bears bad fruit.

Therefore, the Scriptures speak of being "born again" (John 3:7-8) or made "a new creation" (2 Cor. 5:17). The Scriptures speak of God taking out the evil man's "heart of stone" and giving him a "heart of flesh" (Ezek. 11:19-20). Such images are meant to convey this need for a new nature which alone can cause someone to will that which is good. The *Westminster Confession of Faith* describes it as God "enlightening

---

16 *Revisions*, 1.9.4.
17 *On Grace and Free Will*, 31.15, in NPNF, 5:456.

their minds spiritually and savingly to understand the things of God, taking away their heart of stone, and giving unto them a heart of flesh; renewing their wills, and, by his almighty power, determining them to that which is good, and effectually drawing them to Jesus Christ: yet so, as they come most freely, being made willing by his grace."[18] Augustine refers to it as "a secret, wonderful, and ineffable power operating within, that God works in men's hearts not only revelations of the truth, but also good dispositions of the will."[19] Because the nature of all persons is evil from birth, only the direct intervention of God can change us so that we desire and hence "choose" the good. This is why Joel Beeke and Paul Smalley describe regeneration not as "a new choice of the will, but a new creation of the heart, the supernatural gift of a new vital disposition toward God that reorients all the faculties, including the will."[20]

For Pelagius, the will was neutral. It was not bent in any one direction, either good or evil. In this way man is able of his own power to choose good and abstain from evil. "We have implanted in us by God a possibility for acting in both directions…We are born not fully developed, but with a capacity for either conduct; we are formed naturally without either virtue or vice."[21] Circumstances and habit could incline the will in a particular direction, but ultimately it remained autonomous. The will could be "stunned" into action by the good example of Christ and by the terrible sanction of hellfire, but direct interference by God in the conversion of the lost would be tantamount to making God unfair—unless He did it for everyone. Augustine claims that such a view of the free choice of the will is exaggerated "to such a degree that [the Pelagians] leave no place for God's grace, since they insist that it

---

18 Ibid, 10.1.
19 *On the Grace of Christ and Original Sin*, 1.8.
20 Beeke and Smalley, *Reformed Systematic Theology*, Vol. 2 (Wheaton, IL: Crossway, 2020), 429.
21 Pelagius, *Defense of the Freedom of the Will*, 2.14.

is bestowed according to our merits."[22]

Such a view is problematic in numerous ways when it comes to evangelism methodology. For instance, Brown notices it was Pelagianism which "inevitably placed a great emphasis on the fear of punishment."[23] This is a remarkable observation in several ways. First, he describes it as "inevitable," something that necessarily comes about from such a doctrine. It is typically Augustine's doctrine of predestination that is seen as harsh or cold, while Pelagius' view is viewed as optimistic and gracious. But Brown (who is no Augustinian in the theological sense) observes "a cold streak in the mentality of the whole Pelagian movement," while Augustine comes across as more charitable.[24] How can we account for this?

Augustine, the Minister of Grace

For the Pelagian, Adam was less to blame for his sin than we are for ours, "for he had not the great benefit of the previous execution of a human being to deter him."[25] Pelagius thought doing the right thing is merely a matter of will-power and gusto. If you want to do the right thing, you will do it. That is why there is little grace or understanding given to those who do the wrong thing. They are expected to do what is right since their will is neutral, whereas for Augustine, the lost man can't do what is right, since their will is bent toward evil.

This is why Augustine would often write of Christ as the great Physician of sick souls: "There was no reason for the coming of Christ the Lord except to save sinners. Take away diseases, take away wounds, and there is no reason for medicine. If the great Physician came from

---

22 *Revisions*, 1.9.3.
23 Brown, *Augustine of Hippo*, 374.
24 Ibid.
25 Ibid.

heaven, a great sick man was lying ill through the whole world. That sick man is the human race."[26] Such thinking was rejected by the Pelagius concept of man, as was Augustine's comment, "He who says, 'I am not a sinner,' or 'I was not,' is ungrateful to the Savior. No one of men in that mass of mortals which flows down from Adam, no one at all of men is not sick: no one is healed without the grace of Christ."[27] In the same sermon Augustine proclaims, "Nothing is ours except the sin that we have."[28] Because of sin, "the whole mass of the human race [was] alienated from God by Adam," and thus the necessity for the Incarnation.[29] In another sermon Augustine argues, "From Adam we too were born and as the Apostle says, 'In Adam all die…' While healthy, we disregarded his orders, and we tasted from experience how deadly an injury it was to disregard His orders. We began to get sick, we were in pain, we lay in our sickbed, but we must not get discouraged. So because we were not able to go to the doctor, He himself deigned to come to us. Though he was disregarded by the healthy, He did not disregard the wounded."[30] We see here how the image of the minister as the "physician of souls" takes its form from Augustine and other church fathers.

But why is it "Pelagius, not Augustine, who harps on the terrors of the Last Judgement?"[31] Augustine was not averse to the topic of hell, as Brown himself notes: "Augustine knew how to play on an audience's fear of Hell."[32] Augustine's preaching of hell could even elicit scenes similar to those under Jonathan Edwards over a thousand years later: "They were so identified with his feelings, that they would even burst

---

26 Sermon, 175.1.
27 Ibid, 176.2.
28 Ibid, 176.6.
29 Ibid, 293.
30 Ibid, 88.7.
31 Brown, *Augustine of Hippo*, 374.
32 Ibid, 243.

into sudden shouts of terror at an abrupt mention of the wrath of God."[33] Augustine often attributed the afflictions and woes of this life to "the wrath of God."[34] Augustine was not hesitant to evoke dread in his hearers: "We really must be afraid my brothers and sisters. We're exultant now, rejoicing, cheering. I beg you: let that day find you all ready. The one who is saying these things is not lying, he has never lied; if you are still not sure about that, take care that perhaps what he says may be true."[35] The gospel calls out to men everywhere to repent: "Certainly, the word of God frightens us out of our wits, the trumpet of the gospel scares us rigid."[36]

The focus for Augustine is different than that of the Pelagians, however. For Augustine, what a person should fear most about hell is the loss of God's presence. "There is only one thing he fears: 'I shall never look at you again.'"[37] "But a sense of the loss of a loved one, not of punishment, is what he wished most to communicate."[38] In contrast, Pelagianism would resort to what is called "shock and awe" tactics to stagger the will into a response. It was a means to an end. It was a type of pragmatism. Augustine's response to such tactics is still appropriate today: "A man who is afraid of sinning because of hell-fire, is afraid, not of sinning, but of burning."[39] For Augustine, coming to Christ to avoid punishment is not the right motive. Coming to Christ to escape hell is not the right motive. The motive for coming to Christ should be Christ, despite the benefits that come with it, namely, the escape from hell and the gain of heaven. The true believer comes to Christ out of love for the Savior. "Do not think you are dragged to God against

---

33 Ibid, 369.
34 *City of God*, 21.24.78.
35 *The Works of Augustine*, III/11, 107.
36 Ibid.
37 Sermon, 164.10.
38 Brown, *Augustine of Hippo*, 243.
39 *Nicene and Post-Nicene Fathers*, Letter 145, 4.

your will. The mind is drawn by love which is a source of inexpressible pleasure. There is a pleasure of the heart whose sweetness consists in the bread of heaven."[40] The Pelagian can't speak of such love, since it is duty and obedience which saves him, not a change of desire.

Augustine's more robust understanding of sin ironically makes him the more compassionate minister since he is more aware of the need of God's intervention in the life of the lost. This in turn brings more glory to God when a person is converted since it was all a work of God's—not partly God's and partly the person's. "Not only the major but even the minor goods cannot exist unless they come from Him from whom all good things come—that is, God."[41] Pelagius ascribes to God many ways in which He helps convince a sinner of his ways, such as "blessings, healings, chastenings and excitements."[42] But Augustine notes one glaring error in the catalogue—God's love for the sinner: "But that He gives us love and helps us in the this way, this you do not say."[43]

For Augustine, God's love does not mean He made men in a certain way and then left them to themselves when it came to their conversion. It also doesn't mean God is helplessly standing on the sidelines, rooting for people to come to Him, wringing His hands, but refusing to get involved in any kind of inward way. Rather, God's love means He actively intervenes in the inward life of His people and saves them, since nothing else could have done the job. People "could not, of themselves, choose to love."[44] Conversion then is truly a miracle and gift from God. This is the crux of the matter that divides Augustine from Pelagius, and the consequences as it pertains to evangelism could

---

40 *TJ* 26.4.
41 *Free Choice*, 2.19.50.
42 Brown, *Augustine of Hippo*, 374.
43 Ibid.
44 Ibid, 375.

not be greater.

Advantages of Augustinian Evangelism

Augustine clearly believes that even though lost men have natures inclined to evil, Christ must still be offered to sinners in order for them to believe. This is God's way of doing evangelism. The elect will hear the gospel and believe it. Christ alone can deliver the enslaved from their shackles of sin, as he did in a physical sense for the Israelites who were in bondage in Egypt. We must not worry about whom God has chosen, but rather call all men everywhere to come to him. However, there are several distinctives of Augustinian evangelism that make it more favorable—and biblical—than Pelagianism.

Augustine's view of God and man protect him from two mindsets that Pelagians often fall prey to.[45] This is not to say the Augustinian view will always be free from such dangers, but it is to say that, if consistent, it won't be a threat. The first danger is discouragement, and with discouragement comes the tendency to use pragmatism and gimmicks in evangelism. The person who holds to Augustinian soteriology believes God alone grants regeneration to the unbeliever. If people aren't being saved, the Augustinian won't need to resort to trickery, shock and awe, or a watered-down message since it wouldn't help anyway. They won't think that since simple gospel proclamation isn't working, they need to try something else. Nor will the person be discouraged, seeing conversion is God's work, not ours, and that God has promised to save His sheep. God has promised to build His church. Our job is to be faithful in sharing the gospel. God's work is to convert sinners.

But the Pelagian, not seeing anyone saved through simple gospel

---

45 For a fuller treatment of this topic, see Ryan Denton, *Even if None: Reclaiming Biblical Evangelism* (San Francisco, Calif.: First Love Publications, 2019) and *10 Modern Evangelism Myths: A Biblical Corrective* (Grand Rapids, MI: Reformation Heritage Books, 2021).

proclamation, will feel pressure to get the person converted. Since gospel preaching did not work, he must now resort to a different tactic. This is why the Pelagian message about hell comes across so callously. They must "stun" the will into action if simple gospel preaching fails to work. At the very least, if the person is not stunned into action, the Pelagian will become discouraged and put the blame on himself for not seeing others saved. Will Metzger shows this in *Tell the Truth*: "A clear understanding that success in evangelism is a result of God's initiating grace frees the evangelist from false guilt when conversions have not happened."[46] Or the one evangelizing will become cold or bitter towards the person he is evangelizing, putting the blame on the sinner for not being saved. He thinks he himself, the Pelagian, could believe the gospel and stop sinning, so why can't the other person?

Just as dangerous is the second difference that results from these differing views of soteriology. In the Augustinian view, if someone is saved through a person's gospel efforts, the person knows it was God alone who did it, not the one being witnessed to or the one witnessing. It wasn't the person's speech, his holy life, his wisdom, or anything else—it was God who had mercy (Rom. 9:16). On the contrary, the Pelagian must to some extent believe it was the person's decision or belief that saved him, not God's unconditional election. God made the person savable but the person took the initiative to do the rest upon hearing the gospel. Such a mindset leads to pride in the one converted, since he is the one who believed, and pride in the one sharing the gospel, since he did so in such a way that the unbeliever accepted it.

The Augustinian view lessens the temptation of thinking the Christian has anything to do with someone's salvation, apart from sharing the gospel with them. The Christian will recall he is preaching to dry

---

46 Metzger, *Tell the Truth* (Downers Grove, IL: InterVarsity, 1981), 163.

bones and that "the wicked, through the pride of his countenance, will not seek after God: God is not in all his thoughts" (Ps. 10:4). Louis Berkhof notes this when referring to Calvin's own approach to evangelism, which was influenced by Augustine: "According to Calvin the gospel call is not in itself effective but is made efficacious by the operation of the Holy Spirit, when He savingly applies the Word to the heart of man; and it is so applied only in the hearts and lives of the elect. Thus, the salvation of man remains the work of God from the very beginning."[47]

For Augustine, any fruit or salvific success from evangelism can't be attributed to the Christian, since salvation "*is not of him who wills, nor of him who runs, but of God who shows mercy*" (Rom. 9:16). If the Christian sees bones rattle to life, he will know he was sharing the gospel with a dead man. He will know it is no credit of his that someone was raised to "newness of life" (Rom. 6:4). He will glorify God, not his own ability, since it was God who was "ready to be sought by those who did not ask for Me; I was ready to be found by those who did not seek Me" (Isa. 65:1). Augustine asks in a work against Pelagius, "How many of Christ's enemies at the present day are being suddenly drawn by a secret grace?"[48] In ways unknown to the human eye, God is working in His elect through the preaching of the gospel, calling them, saving them.

This does not mean the Christian should not study to show himself "approved" (2 Tim. 2:15). It does not mean the Christian should be sloppy or uncouth in his delivery of the gospel. It does not mean the Christian should leave off pleading with the lost to turn to Christ. It does not mean the Christian should not live in a way that is consistent with the gospel he proclaims. It means God is the agent of a person's

---

47 Louis Berkhof, *Systematic Theology* (Carlisle, PA: The Banner of Truth, 1958), 459.
48 1.19.37.

salvation, and hence God alone deserves all the glory. Without this understanding the Christian will try to entice the person's emotions in unbiblical ways. This is why the Pelagian will attempt to speak cleverly, callously, or try to trick an unbeliever in order to "draw" him to Christ.

Augustine's view provides great comfort to the Christian since it is not up to him to save sinners. He can't, in fact. He is called to share the gospel, but it is God who gives the increase. The Christian does not need to rely on props or tricks when it comes to evangelism since "the natural man receiveth not the things of the Spirit of God: for they are foolishness unto him: neither can he know them, because they are spiritually discerned" (1 Cor. 2:14). God is sovereign in salvation and man is incapable of being "born again" apart from God's regenerating grace. Thus, the Christian can go out in total dependence on God. He will be liberated from the burden of "saying the right thing" or the fear of "saying the wrong thing." He cannot push people "further" away from God. The believer can trust in God to do what He wishes with the gospel.

Augustine's Sympathetic Evangelism

This is why Augustine seems to have more freedom to speak on topics such as love even in the context of hell. Augustine comes across as more sympathetic to the plight of his fellow men. For the Pelagians, "man had no excuse for his own sins, nor for the evils around him."[49] The reason for man's sins was external to his "true self," and thus, man's habits could be changed by mere exertion of the will. Such a view of man leaves little dependency on God when evangelizing, since conversion itself is no longer overtly supernatural or spiritual. For Augustine, the opposite is the case. Because of man's radical depravity, the Lord alone

---

49 Brown, *Augustine of Hippo*, 357.

can intervene and give them a new nature. This is why regeneration must precede faith, and also why faith itself is a gift from God. "No one believes who is not called. God calls in his mercy, and not as rewarding the merits of faith. The merits of faith follow his calling rather than precede it…Unless, therefore, the mercy of God in calling precedes, no one can even believe, and so begin to be justified and to receive power to do good works. So grace comes before all merits. Christ died for the ungodly."[50] In his *Revisions*, Augustine explains: "And this divine gift whereby [the will] is freed would be given because of its merits and would not be grace, which is certainly freely given, unless the divine gift preceded it."[51] Applying this to the Romans 9 passage about Jacob and Esau, Augustine affirms it was God who chose Jacob and passed over Esau, since God alone could have done something about Esau's impenitent heart: "Who would dare to affirm that the omnipotent lacked a method of persuading even Esau to believe?"[52]

The handicap of Pelagianism in contrast to Augustinianism is apparent theologically and practically, as Augustine demonstrates in his writings. But the significance of this topic as it relates to evangelism demands we deal with it in more detail in the next chapter, looking especially at why predestination is a doctrine "for fighting men."

50 *To Simplican—On Various Questions, Book 1*, tr. J. H. S. Burleigh in *Augustine: Earlier Writings*. Philadelphia, 1953, 2.7.
51 *Revisions*, 1.9.4.
52 *To Simplican—On Various Questions, Book 1*, 2.14.

Other Evangelism Benefits Accruing from Predestination

Augustine's views on predestination were challenged by more than just Pelagians. Prosper and Hilary, two monks in southern Gaul, thought men were "free to respond to this challenge [of conversion] of their own free will."[1] Augustine's views of man appeared to them as "the blackest pessimism." They would point to the advance of the gospel in their own day as proof that Augustine was in error. "Christianity had come to the tribes that had entered the Roman Empire from the North; in this generation, it will spill over into Scotland and Ireland. The response of utterly foreign peoples to the message of Christianity reassured men that God 'wishes all men to be saved.'"[2]

Interestingly, this was the same data Augustine himself was looking at to conclude that his position on man and the gospel was the correct one. The gracious God had saved people out of every tribe, tongue and nation by giving them new natures, which in turn prompted them to

---

1 Brown, *Augustine of Hippo*, 403.
2 Ibid, 403-404.

turn to Christ. The fact so many foreign peoples were being saved was exactly Augustine's point. Considering how evil and self-seeking human beings are, how else could one account for their conversion except by pointing to God's utter grace and power in salvation? Augustine believed "his giddy doctrine of predestination…was merely another 'impregnable bastion' of the Catholic faith."[3] He admitted the doctrine was difficult and open to abuse, but Peter had said as much of the ideas of Paul. Peter did not criticize Paul for his difficult ideas but rather blamed "the men who had willfully misunderstood these truths."[4] Augustine's followers, which eventually would include Prosper the monk, would call themselves "lovers of all-or-nothing grace." Any other position could not claim an absolute dependence on the grace of God for conversion. Men like Pelagius "place the initiative in their salvation on a wrong footing by placing it in themselves."[5] Therefore, "all-or-nothing grace" was exactly that. If man contributes anything to their own salvation, it is not grace. B. B. Warfield states about Augustine, "His doctrine of grace was all his own: it represented the very core of his being."[6] But it was not merely a "doctrine of grace" that represented Augustine's position. It was the necessity of grace. For Pelagius grace existed, but only to the extent that God creates man with a neutral will and provides examples of good conduct through the law, first, and the good example of Christ, second. There is no internal change done to the person to make them believe the gospel.

Two things made Augustine aware of the necessity of God's grace—his own experience as an unbeliever and the message of the Scriptures, which show that the whole human race was in Adam when he fell, and consequently, the human race is partaker in Adam's guilt

---

3 Brown, *Augustine of Hippo*, 405.
4 *Nicene and Post-Nicene Fathers*, Letter, 214, 6-7.
5 Brown, *Augustine of Hippo*, 406.
6 B. B. Warfield, *Studies in Tertullian and Augustine*, 322.

and condemnation. "Sin came into the world through one man, and death through sin, and so death spread to all men because all sinned… by the one man's disobedience the many were made sinners" (Rom. 5:12,19). Warfield describes such a consequence as follows: "The result of this is that we have lost the divine image, though not in such a sense that no lineaments of it remain to us; and, the sinning soul making the flesh corruptible, our whole nature is corrupted, and we are unable to do anything of ourselves truly good."[7] Apart from being born again, man is corrupt and under the power of Satan. "As it is written, There is none righteous, no, not one: There is none that understandeth, there is none that seeketh after God. They are all gone out of the way, they are together become unprofitable; there is none that doeth good, no, not one" (Rom. 3:10-12). The will "is now injured, wounded, diseased, enslaved."[8] For Augustine,

> Man's dilemma is that when he has seen what he ought to do, his will is too weak to do it. The will is indeed in working order for making choices, but the preferred choices are for whatever is comfortable and pleasurable. Hence the problem if the very nature of man, ever restless, ever seeking happiness in places where it cannot be found, knowing not only that he is sick at heart but that he is the very cause of his own sickness.[9]

Hence the necessity for divine grace. The will, though free, doesn't have the power to do good. Man is wholly incapable of turning to the Lord apart from God supernaturally giving them a new nature. The will can "will" the good only when the person's nature is changed by God. This is what Paul means when he says we are a new creature or

---

7 B. B. Warfield, "The Origin and Nature of Pelagianism," 90.
8 Ibid, 91.
9 Chadwick, *Augustine: A Very Short Introduction*, 67.

creation in Christ (2 Cor. 5:17). We now desire and fear the God we once hated. We now hate and fear the sin we once loved. This is what Jesus called "the new birth" (John 3:3).

A Doctrine for Fighting Men

Augustine saw predestination as "a doctrine for fighting men."[10] Because men were predestined to believe the gospel, Christians became "the agents of forces which guaranteed achievements greater than their own frail efforts could have ever brought about."[11] Far from sapping evangelistic energy, "a doctrine of predestination divorced from action was inconceivable to Augustine."[12] Prosper the monk would say, "the elect receive grace, not to allow them to be idle, but to enable them to work well."[13] Amazingly, Brown calls this "as good a summary as any of the most immediate legacy of Augustine to the making of early medieval Europe."[14] The doctrine of predestination invigorated men to serve the Lord in the face of all difficulties. Augustine's life was a living embodiment of this truth and here we discover why—he was guaranteed success. There was the absolute certainty of belonging to a mission whose purpose would prove effective.[15] The Lord will give weak men strength to do great deeds, and the Lord will make sure evil men get converted. "No subject gives me greater pleasure. For what ought to be more attractive to us sick men, than grace, grace by which we are healed; for us lazy men, than grace, grace by which we are stirred up; for us men longing to act, than grace, by which we are helped?"[16]

---

10 Brown, *Augustine of Hippo*, 406.
11 Ibid.
12 Ibid.
13 Prosper, *de vocatione omnium gentium*, 2.35.
14 Brown, *Augustine of Hippo*, 513.
15 Ibid, 406.
16 *Nicene and Post-Nicene Fathers*, Letter, 186.

Some think belief in the doctrine of God's unconditional election will produce a lack of zeal in evangelism, but history shows the opposite: "This doctrine does not hinder the work of mission, but powerfully energizes it. Through the preaching of men the elect will be gathered in. Therefore, the gospel must be preached by men!"[17] Wes Bredenhof observes that "even when the mission work of the church does not appear successful from a human perspective, God's purposes will never be frustrated. Whether through one missionary or another, whether through one sermon or another, through whatever means He chooses, God will gather His elect."[18]

This is further confirmed when we look at religious groups influenced by Augustinian doctrine, particularly the Reformers and Post-Reformers of the sixteenth and seventeenth centuries. Historian Carlos Eire, in many ways unsympathetic to the Reformed movement, admits "Calvinists did not just theorize; they were also eager to overthrow false religion and any ruler who defended it."[19] Also, "Calvinists tended to be aggressive, impatient, and bent on continual growth. And wherever they surfaced, their activism would kick into high gear."[20] Predestination did not quench evangelistic fire, but rather was like gasoline. Eire records that Calvinism spread to Scotland, England, Germany, Hungary, Poland and Lithuania within the span of fifty or so years.[21]

But what does "Calvinism" have to do with Augustine? Martin Luther had been an Augustinian friar and John Calvin's *Institutes*, one of the most popular books of Reformation Europe, quotes Augustine more than anyone else. Also, many North American Puritans were

---

17 Wes Bredenhof, *To Win Our Neighbors for Christ* (Grand Rapids: Reformation Heritage, 2012), 82.
18 Ibid, 83.
19 Carlos M. N. Eire, *Reformations* (New Haven, CT: Yale University, 2016), 312.
20 Ibid.
21 Ibid, 312-314.

concerned for the salvation of the natives among whom they resided, and from the time of the earliest arrivals in the New World there was discussion and activity about how to reach the natives with the gospel. The Puritans were so influenced by John Calvin that they were called "English Genevans."[22] But to be influenced by John Calvin inevitably meant they were influenced by Augustine on this issue, whether or not they were conscious of it (most of them were).

Assurance of Faith

Such a doctrine had other benefits for believers that Pelagius could never claim, such as the perseverance of the saints. Augustine taught that Christians should humbly look to Christ all their life, prayerfully asking God for the grace to persevere. Augustine believed that a Christian can't know for certain if he is of the elect, but rather than be spiritually apathetic, it should produce in us a humble zeal to always look to Christ until the end of our pilgrimage. On the surface, Augustine's view does not provide much as far as assurance of salvation goes, but because of his robust view of predestination, he is very much aware that God alone can preserve the Christian's faith to the end of life. There is a definite number of elect saints who will persevere. "The elect can never know for certain whether or not they are elect... There could be only one empirical test of election, and that a necessary but not a sufficient test, namely perseverance to one's last breath, dying in a state of grace."[23] In this way, election is no ground for presumption. To persevere in faith and repentance until the time of one's death is a sign that one is elect.

This is one explanation for why predestination became so attractive

---

22 Patrick Collinson, "Antipuritanism," *Cambridge Companion to Puritanism*, ed. by John Coffey and Paul C. H. Lin (Cambridge: University Press, 2008), 22.
23 Chadwick, *Augustine: A Very Short Introduction*, 124.

among the Church of Augustine's day. "The idea that a divine decree had already established 'an unshakeable number of the elect,' that the sons of God were 'permanently ascribed in the archive of the Father' was desperately welcomed; for it provided men with what he knew they could never create for themselves: a permanent core of identity, mysteriously free from those vertiginous chasms whose presence in the soul he had always felt so acutely."[24] The believer would be preserved by God to maintain their love and trust in Christ, while also feeling a disgust for sin. In this way, the survival and spread of the church was guaranteed, because the salvation and spiritual survival of the elect was guaranteed. Christ would not let His sheep fall away. "The elect received this gift so that they, also, could tread the hard way of Christ."[25] In its deepest sense, "it was a doctrine of survival, a fierce insistence that God alone could provide man with an irreducible inner core," but this is exactly what made it so potent a force in evangelism.

The Pelagian doctrine did not guarantee evangelistic success, which is why, then as now, it resorted to either bait and switch, pragmatism, or scare tactics to be "effective." They were largely on their own when it came to the salvation of sinners. God was not going to directly intervene. For the Pelagian, if someone was converted or maintained such conversion until his death, such a person could glory in himself as much as he does in God, since the person had as much to do with his own salvation as did God. For Augustine, predestination and man's evil nature made certain that anyone converted could only glory "in a sense of agency found on God."[26] Only the "gravity of love" could hold people to the end, and only God could put such love into the hearts of people who once warred against Him.[27]

---

24 Brown, *Augustine of Hippo*, 408.
25 Ibid, 409.
26 Ibid, 512.
27 *Confessions*, Tr. Philip Burton (London: Everyman's Library, 2001), 13.9.10.

The *Belgic Confession* describes something similar in Article XXIV: "We believe that this true faith, being wrought in man by the hearing of the Word of God and the operation of the Holy Ghost, doth regenerate and make him a new man, causing him to live a new life, and freeing him from the bondage of sin."[28] Faith is wrought in man through the hearing of the gospel and the effectual application of it by the Holy Spirit. It is that simple. Throughout church history, beginning in Adam's day, the Holy Spirit applying the proclamation of the Word of God is what converts the elect. The *Second London Baptist Confession* states that "the gospel is the only outward means of revealing Christ and saving grace, and it is abundantly sufficient for that purpose."[29] This sentence encapsulates everything that needs to be said regarding biblical evangelism, which is simply revealing Christ's "saving grace" to the lost. Such an approach is certain to be "abundantly sufficient," regardless of salvific results, which is the point that Augustine realized. God will regenerate the elect through the preaching of the gospel. And His elect will make it to the end.

This is what Augustine understood so well, saying in one place, "For as we do not know who belongs to the number of the predestined or who does not belong, we ought to be so minded as to wish that all men be saved."[30] Such a mindset would carry over into the Reformers, the Puritans, Jonathan Edwards and George Whitefield, the great "Missionary Movements" of Hudson Taylor and Adinirom Judson, Charles Spurgeon and countless others who saw what Augustine saw when it came to God's sovereignty in conversion. William Carey provides a remarkable example of this trust in the sovereignty of God in salvation during the early days of ministry in India: "I am

---

28 Much of the rest of this chapter has been developed from a previous book, *10 Modern Evangelism Myths* (Grand Rapids, MI: Reformation Heritage, 2021).
29 2LBC 20:4
30 On *Rebuke and Grace*, Ch. 43.

very fruitless and almost useless but the Word and the attributes of God are my hope, and my confidence, and my joy, and I trust that his glorious designs will undoubtedly be answered."[31] Iain Murray remarks of Carey, "The obstacles were immense. Problems of poverty and illness, overshadowed by the darker burden of a land where in Carey's words, 'ten thousand ministers would find scope for their powers,' were constantly with them. Through the first five and a half years they saw not a single Indian convert."[32] Carey would go on to see revival several years later, but when times were difficult, it was God's sovereignty that buoyed him along. The same was true for Augustine.

Theology Matters in Evangelism

The Pelagian position takes away from the glory of God and leads to pride and false conversions. The Pelagian is always obligated to do all he can to manipulate the will of man into "choosing" God. This kind of evangelism will attempt to attract men with ritzy methods or eloquent and soft-peddled attractions, not the gospel. The notion of libertarian free will as it pertains to salvation is essentially in the same family as the Roman Catholic works-based system. It claims Christ has done His part, now you must do yours. Christ did a little, now you do a little. But if a person has to choose Christ in order to be saved, what does choosing entail? Walking an aisle? Saying a prayer? Raising a hand? Getting baptized? Anything the synergist puts forward will by default make it works-based. "The very reason many contemporary churches embrace pragmatic methodology is that they lack any understanding of God's sovereignty in the salvation of the elect. They lose confidence in the power of the preached gospel to reach hardened unbelievers.

---

31 William Carey to Mary Carey and Ann Hobson, December 22, 1796, in *The Journal and Selected Letters of William Carey*, ed. Terry G. Carter (Macon, GA: Smyth & Helwys, 2000), 249.
32 Iain H. Murray, *The Puritan Hope* (Carlisle, PA: The Banner of Truth, 1971), 140.

That's why they approach evangelism as a marketing problem."[33] The Bible shows man is saved because God gives them a new heart (Ezek. 36:26), and in doing so, man repents and believes the gospel. God raises the spiritually dead to life. God loosens the shackles of sin. The only choice when it comes to salvation is God's, and rightly so. Christ prayed, "Thy will be done" (Matt. 6:10), not man's, because man's will is undone—thus God alone can change the situation.

Consider Jesus' great lesson on evangelism. He goes to the disciples after they had toiled all night for fish but caught nothing. They are tired and discouraged. He tells them to cast the net on the other side of the boat. Peter even complains, "But we've fished all night and caught nothing" (Luke 5:5). Peter is here implying that having seen no success previously, there won't be any success the next time either. But despite the protest, off they go, throwing the net out on the other side. They did not say to Jesus, "But you're a carpenter, not a fisherman!" They did not fold their arms and walk home. They knew who the Lord of the Harvest was. They trusted His sovereignty and they obeyed His orders. This is the epitome of Augustinian evangelism. Notice the apostles didn't try anything differently, either. They did not need to modify or reinvent the way they had previously gone about it. Using the same method, they were blessed with a great catch.

This is what the sovereignty of God in evangelism promises. If we don't see fruit, we don't need to modify or change the gospel. We don't need to water it down or hide unpleasant truths. We don't need to stun the will into a decision. We certainly don't need to quit. We know the Lord will honor the biblical method of evangelism—gospel proclamation and prayer. And trusting Him, we can go out with confidence, knowing He oversees whether fish come into the net or not. But He

---

33 MacArthur, *Ashamed of the Gospel*, (Wheaton, IL: Crossway Books, 1993), 167.

has promised us they will come, and for two thousand years now it has happened.

Augustine's Evangelism to Pagans

Henry Chadwick has noted that the Latin word *paganus* conveys the idea of a "civilian," in contrast to a soldier. In Augustine's day, Christians used the word "pagan" to describe non-Christians who had not by baptism entered the fray of war against the world, the flesh and the devil. They were not soldiers of Christ.[1] Hence they were pagans, or civilians.

Christian evangelism to pagans was an early fact in the church. Paul's most memorable sermon is arguably the one delivered in Athens on Mar's Hill to a group of pagans, philosophers, and other Gentile unbelievers (Acts 17). But in Augustine's day, Christians had failed to convert the barbarian tribes beyond the frontiers. They did not even try.[2] The barbarians were converted when they entered the Roman Empire and adopted Roman ways of life, which included taking on the official religion at the time, Christianity.[3]

---

1 *Augustine of Hippo: A Life*, 123.
2 Brown, *Religion and Society*, 148.
3 Ibid.

This failure to evangelize the tribes beyond the frontiers is likely because of the social cleavage between the Christians and the barbarians at the time. The cultural gulf between them was simply too great. Another factor was a lack of infrastructure to enable the church to expand outwardly in an intentional manner. The church lacked the means to expand by missionary activity.[4] Another explanation was the utter inability to even conceive of such an outreach to people beyond the frontiers. Such a category of thought was simply missing from the minds of Western Christians of the time. This could perhaps be explained by the fact that, at least for a season, many of the barbarian tribes were coming to them in order to be instructed in the Christian faith. Augustine tells of a time when remote tribesmen came down the hill to knock on his door. He asked them what they wanted. "'To know the glory of God,'" they told him.[5] There was not a real need to reach outside the boundaries of the Roman Empire to evangelize the tribesmen since those who were interested would come to them. This is not the biblical model of missions, but we can understand how such a scenario would tempt one's focus to become inward rather than outward. The same could be seen in America in the 1970s and 80s, when inviting a neighbor to church or a revival meeting was all it would take to get the person to hear the gospel. People weren't as reluctant to enter a church building in those days and so the need to go outside the walls of the church to evangelize wasn't as urgent. The same could be said of the so called "seeker friendly" church model, which attempts to create a church atmosphere that appeals to those who are lost, hence eliminating the necessity of going out to them with the gospel.

None of the above approaches are the biblical model of evangelism. Although nothing is wrong with inviting someone to church, the focus

---

4 Ibid.
5 Letter, 134.22.

of evangelism should be outward, with each particular Christian sharing the gospel with the lost people he or she encounters outside the church. Then, upon their conversion, the person will then desire to be in church with the saints. Preaching the gospel from the pulpit is also a valid form of evangelism, but most Christians aren't ministers and so the need to share the gospel outside the church with family, strangers, coworkers and their children is imperative. So is the need for church planting overseas and at home. This is the pattern that we see in the New Testament. To an extent this was happening in Augustine's day, but anything like "foreign missions" was an anomaly. Christians in the twenty-first century are privileged to come after the great revivals and missionary movements of the modern church. We typically understand that the command is to go to the lost, even those in other countries and to those who speak other languages, not for the lost to come to us—as encouraging as it is when they do come. For us, to not evangelize the world seems foreign. In Augustine's day, it was the reverse.

The Conversion of Victorinus

Not all pagans were "barbarians" who lived outside the Roman Empire, however. The pagans Augustine dealt with were those living within the Roman Empire. The conversion of a pagan named Victorinus had a remarkable influence on Augustine's own conversion. Like Augustine, Victorinus was an African who had become a popular orator-philosopher in Rome. Also like Augustine, who had been a sort of evangelist for the Manicheans before his conversion to Christianity, he was an evangelist for the cult of the gods.[6] He was the type of man that the non-Christian Augustine aspired to become. But as an old man Victorinus had been drawn to the Christian faith. He remained un-

---

6 MacMullen, *Christianizing the Roman Empire*, 69.

baptized for a lengthy period of time since doing so would have cost him his friends, job and comfort as a famous orator. At last, he became ashamed of his cowardice and was openly baptized in defiance of Roman paganism. Augustine would describe Victorinus's conversion as

> a glorious proof of thy [God's] grace, which ought to be confessed to thee: how that old man, most learned, most skilled in the liberal arts; who had read, criticized, and explained so many of the writings of the philosophers; the teacher of so many noble senators; one who, as a mark of his distinguished service in office had both merited and obtained a statue in the Roman Forum—which mean of this world esteem a great honor—this man who, up to an old age, had been a worshipper of idols, a communicant in the sacrilegious rites to which almost all the nobility of Rome were wedded...despite all this, he did not blush to become a child of thy Christ, a babe at thy font, bowing his neck to the yoke of humility and submitting his forehead to the ignominy of the cross.[7]

Augustine asks the question, "by what means didst thou find thy way into that breast," which is a poetic way to inquire of the evangelism methodology that was used to save Victorinus.[8] As is typical of Augustine, we see here he is very much concerned with the ways in which people are converted, another indication of his evangelistic passion. Augustine attributes it in part to Victorinus' reading of the Scriptures. He also had a friend, Simplicianus, who would pressure Victorinus to make his faith public—or to "count the cost." But Victorinus "was fearful of offending his friends, proud demon worshippers...He feared

---

7 *Confessions*, 8.2.3.
8 Ibid, 8.2.4.

that a storm of enmity would descend upon him" because of his be-lief in Christ.[9] Once Victorinus' conversion became public, he would be forbidden to teach rhetoric after a law passed by Emperor Julian prohibited Christians from doing so. Augustine notes, "he steadily gained strength from reading and inquiry" and through friends such as Simplicianus, who reminded Victorinus that Christ would deny him before the holy angels if he was afraid to confess Christ before men. Ashamed, Victorinus said, "'Let us go to the church; I wish to become a Christian.'"[10]

Augustine credits God for the conversion of Victorinus, but we see that God uses means such as Scripture and the regular encouragement and even loving rebuke of friends to bring it about. In fact, the story of Victorinus' conversion is told to Augustine by this same Simpli-cianus for the purpose of moving Augustine to imitate him—and it worked![11] When recalling Victorinus' conversion years later, Augustine bursts into praise not only for Victorinus' conversion, but for the less well-known conversions as well: "Are there not many men who, out of a deeper pit of darkness than that of Victorinus, return to thee—who draw near to thee and are illuminated by that light which gives those who receive it power from thee to become thy sons?"[12]

Preaching - A Direct Confrontation with Paganism

During Augustine's life, tensions between Christians and pagans were typically fierce. An open clash between Christians and pagans had already occurred in 382 when a Christian group ordered the removal of a pagan statue from the Senate in Rome. Symmachus, a leading pa-

---

9 Ibid.
10 Ibid.
11 Ibid, 8.5.10.
12 Ibid, 8.4.9.

gan, argued that any deviation from the traditional cult and practice of Rome would prove detrimental to the empire. Although the emperors were typically Christians, most of the upper class was still wedded to polytheistic forms of religion. This would in turn influence the peasants since most of them worked for and wanted to please the aristocrats and landowners. Rome's subsequent fall to the barbarians in 410 A.D. ruptured any cohesion between the two groups. "The Christians were promptly blamed for the disaster and the old charge that Christianity was inimical to the well-being of society gained widespread currency among the pagan population."[13] Such an attitude towards Christianity had always been popular among pagans. If drought or famine plagued a city, it was due to the anger of the gods for permitting Christianity to sprout up among them. "No rain, because of the Christians" had become a popular phrase by the mid-fourth century, and the mindset would prevail into the fifth century as well.[14]

Augustine's climate was permeated with paganism so naturally such scapegoating would be attractive to many people. "A sense of the uncanny powers of the gods, fed by stories of miracles performed by their ancient worshippers, still towered above the average Christian."[15] This is clear from the fact that pagan sages had remained heroes in Roman culture.[16] Each city still had its own protecting god or goddess. And yet, far from being hostile towards the pagans, Augustine was eager to see them converted. He told his congregation that the Christians should not destroy the pagans' shrines. They should not invade pagan estates. They should first rid the paganism from their enemy's heart. "Pray for them," he urged. "Do not be angry with them."[17]

---

13 Fortin, "St. Augustine," *History of Political Philosophy*, 176-205.
14 Lane Fox, *Pagans and Christians* (New York, 1987), 137.
15 Brown, *Augustine of Hippo*, 458.
16 Ibid.
17 Sermon 62.11.17.

Because Augustine's congregation would have been exposed to the influences of paganism, much of his evangelism depended on preaching: "Hence the importance of a long sermon 'Against the Pagans,' and a series of similar, shorter sermons preached to congregations that included pagan hearers."[18] His "Against the Pagans" sermon was two and a half hours long, apparently for the purpose of keeping the congregation in church and away from the pagan celebrations being held at the same time.[19] Historians have called it "the jewel of the Mayence collection," a reference to a group of Augustine's works discovered in the late twentieth century.[20] In it Augustine warns his hearers, "If then you wish to mingle with the heathen, you do not wish to follow him who redeemed us. You are mingled then in your life, in your deeds, in your heart by hoping such things, believing such things, and loving such things You are ungrateful to your redeemer, nor do you acknowledge the price he paid, the blood of the immaculate lamb. In order to follow the one who redeemed you with his blood, do not mingle with the heathen in likeness of the morality and the deeds."[21] He brings this point to a close with an exhortation that could have come from a Whitefield or Spurgeon: "If they commit themselves to earthly events, you commit yourselves to the words of the divine scriptures. If they run to the theatre, you run to the church. If they get drunk, you fast. If truly you do these things, then truly you chanted: 'Save us, O Lord our God, and gather us from among the nations.'"[22]

Against the Pagans is truly a quintessential sermon of Augustine's, especially for its evangelistic emphasis. He spends the first part of the sermon applying the song the congregation had just sung to the con-

---

18 Brown, *Augustine of Hippo*, 457.
19 Six-Means, *Augustine and Catholic Christianization*, 145.
20 Brown, *Augustine of Hippo*, 457.
21 Dolbeu 198, 26.2.
22 Ibid.

text of the pagan feast day going on at the same time: "This is what you were singing, after all: *Save us, Lord our God, and gather us from among the nations, that we may confess your holy name.*" Augustine emphasizes that if Christ is their redeemer, then it will be demonstrated by the differences between what the Christians and pagans believe, hope and love. "What after all could be so widely separated as that they believe demons are gods, you believe in the God who is the true God? That they hope for the vanities of this age, you hope for eternal life? That they love the world, you love the world's architect?"[23] This is how the Lord gathers His people from the nations. They are still intermingled among the nations physically, but they are distinct by their lifestyle, thinking, and motives: "They believe that; as for you, believe this. They hope for that; as for you, hope for this. They love that; as for you, love this…They entertain themselves with lascivious songs; as for you, entertain yourselves with words of the scriptures."

The similarities between the pagans in Augustine's day and the unbelievers in our own is striking. Biblical preachers everywhere will be able to note similar themes and emphases in their own sermons, addressed to their own congregations. The songs of the world, the mayhem and obscenity of movies, the celebration of binge drinking or marijuana, the deluge of pornography—such influences are a real threat to our devotion to Christ, even for those who are in the church. Hence the need for addressing these issues in the context of expository preaching. This was Augustine's concern as well, and like a faithful preacher he does not shy away from challenging his hearers.

Augustine not only encourages his congregation to fast for the conversion of the pagans, but to do so as well for the "bad Christians." He cries out, "If only it were just the pagans we had to wring our hands

---

23 Ibid, 198.2.

over! We would then be wringing them for practically nobody."[24] Especially in America, where a vast amount of people still identifies with some form of Christianity, we can appreciate Augustine's sentiment. The pagans were not the only ones guilty of going to the theaters, which were as lewd as an average movie or television show in our own day—but many professing Christians were also caught up in it. Many professing Christians were regularly getting drunk. Many were in peril of dying apart from Christ. Augustine ends the sermon by pointing his hearers to Christ, "the mediator in whom are hidden all the treasures of wisdom and knowledge."[25]

This is one of Augustine's gifts that comes through more and more as he grasps the doctrine of total depravity and God's unconditional election. He realizes that ultimately there is no difference between the pagans and the false Christians. Both need grace. Both are in a state of slavery to sin. But God, being rich in mercy, can save both pagan and false Christian for the sake of His own glory and praise, if only they would call upon the name of the Lord. In another sermon Augustine pleads with his pagan hearers: "Now turn your attention to the salvation doctor who has come to us, our Lord Jesus Christ. He found us blind of heart, he promised us a light which eye has not seen nor ear heard, nor has it come up into the heart of man (1 Cor. 2:9)."[26] He urges, "So don't make your own the cawing of procrastination, but the moaning of confession."[27] Elsewhere he implores, "Keep from going with detestable inquiries to astrologers, to soothsayers, to fortune-tellers, to augurs, to sacrilegious rites of divination," and "if you used to haunt astrologers and other such sacrilegious pests, give it up from now

---

24 Ibid, 198.8.
25 Ibid, 198.62.
26 Sermon 360B, *Works of Augustine*, III/11, 373.
27 Ibid, 381.

on."[28]

In another sermon preached in AD 404, Augustine aims his argument at Christians who are living among pagan neighbors. He claims they must be willing to sacrifice for those still in sin, referring to pagans.[29] "What was it that your Lord did for you, before you were a Christian? He suffered for you."[30] Christ suffered for those still in sin so they could be reconciled to God. Christians must suffer for their pagan neighbors, therefore, even going so far as fasting for them. "What a tiny little test this is! Still, it does reveal how Christian the heart is that beats in your breast."[31] When Augustine senses stirring in the congregation, he responds: "You're now listening to the sermon; you're all ears, you're being stimulated by the word of God, and this very exhortation is beginning to glow in your heart. I have kindled something in your spirits; I can see it, I acknowledge it."[32]

Compassion for the pagans must not stay pent up in the Christian's heart, however. It must drive the Christian to practice. "If you rightly understand what you are hearing, I am quite sure that you are grieving for those who are still caught up in this insanity [paganism]. You are grieving over them because you too, once upon a time, were perhaps caught up in this sort of insanity."[33] How could they forget their pagan neighbors when they too were once lost? They should "feel sorry for them" and "weep."[34] However, they should also have hope. If God saved those hearing this sermon, he can save pagans as well. "You must pray for them. But in order that your prayer may be heard, fast for them and give alms, and for your part spend the day like that on behalf of those

---

28 *Essential Sermons*, Tr. Hill, 41.
29 Dolbeu Sermon 198, *Works of Augustine*, III/11, 184.
30 Ibid.
31 Ibid.
32 Ibid.
33 Ibid, 186.
34 Ibid.

you love."[35] Later Augustine laments, "We must always grieve over them, indeed, as long as they are pagans, as long as they pursue their futile vanities, as long as they are devoted to demons. As long as they are determined to worship what they have made, forgetful of the one by whom they were made, we must always continue to wring our hands over them."[36] Such compassion should come naturally to believers who also once lived in such darkness. He reminds them, "When you were not what you are now, the Church had compassion on you."[37]

Biblical Contextualization

A letter Augustine wrote in 408 A.D. to Paulinus and Therasia demonstrates how intensely Augustine contemplated evangelism to pagans, aware of the need for biblical contextualization before "contextualization" became a buzzword. "The whole question which perplexes men like myself is this—how we ought to live among or for the welfare of those who have not yet learned to live by dying, by turning themselves with a certain mental resolution away from the attractions of mere natural things."[38]

He is speaking here of the lost. The Christians are those who have already learned "to live by dying." They are to be set apart to Christ. Christians should strive to be dead to the passions and attractions of this world. However, this becomes complicated whenever we evangelize people who have not yet died to the world. Such people are still ensnared by the glamor and pomp of life. They do the things we used to do. Thus, evangelizing them will tempt us to compromise since it requires us to enter their worlds. We will need to spend time with

---

35 Ibid.
36 Ibid.
37 Ibid.
38 *Nicene and Post-Nicene Fathers*, Letter 95, 2.

them. We will have to be around sin. In doing so, we may be hooked again by the world and its lusts.

> For in most cases, it seems to us that unless we in some small degree conform to them in regard to those very things from which we desire to see them delivered, we shall not succeed in doing them any good. And when we do thus conform, a pleasure in such things steals upon ourselves, so that often we are pleased to speak and to listen to frivolous things, and not only to smile at them, but even to be completely overcome with laughter: thus burdening our souls with feelings which cleave to the dust, or even to the mire of this world, we experience greater difficulty and reluctance in raising ourselves to God that by dying a gospel-death we may live a gospel-life.[39]

But Augustine never sounds the alarm of retreat. He does not toss in the towel. He does not say we dare not evangelize, then, since we will be tempted to wobble in our striving against sin. But neither is he saying to acquiesce and give ourselves over to the world. He is not saying to compromise. He is not saying to sin. Rather he has a healthy recognition of how complicated evangelism can be. This is a safeguard against heedlessly rushing into evangelism without weighing the risks. The people we seek to see saved are often in messy situations. They are enslaved to lusts. To evangelize them will expose us to temptation, but the call to evangelize does not allow us to flee from such risks. "Behold whence it comes that our whole life on earth is a temptation; for man is tempted even in that thing in which he is being conformed so far as he can be to the likeness of the heavenly life."[40]

---

39 Ibid.
40 Ibid.

What motivated Augustine in his dealings with paganism was similar to his motives when engaging the Donatists. He is confident that the gospel is for anyone who turns to Christ, be they Donatists, Manicheans, worldly Christians, or pagans. "Augustine wished his audience to be certain of one thing—that the Catholic church was "universal" in the most literal sense of the word."[41] He would emphasize that "the way of Christ was open to all."[42]

Correspondence with Pagans

Augustine would also write letters to pagans exhorting them to read the Scriptures. As a layman he was already exchanging letters with lost pagans, exhorting them to become Christian. One such Pagan was a man named Maximus who replied to Augustine in a fashion typical to what Christians hear today—are not all religions one and the same? Polytheism suits him. Christianity suits Augustine. Why pester each other about it?

On another occasion Augustine wrote to a pagan nobleman named Volusianus: "I beg to exhort you, as earnestly as I can, not to grudge to devote attention to the study of the Writings which are truly and unquestionably holy...I exhort you especially to read the writings of the apostles, for from them you will receive a stimulus to acquaint yourself with the prophets, whose testimonies the apostles use."[43] Not stopping there, however, Augustine is quick to let the recipient know that he himself will help him with any questions that come up during his reading: "If in your reading or meditation on what you have read any question arises to the solution of which I may appear necessary,

---

41 Brown, *Augustine of Hippo*, 459.
42 Ibid.
43 Letter 132.

write to me, that I may write in reply."[44]

Augustine received a response to this letter from one of Volusianus's counselors. The counselor is pleased by Augustine's "strenuous effort to establish and hold up the steps of one who is somewhat hesitating," speaking about Volusianius, whose lack of commitment to the faith was a concern to certain people close to him. The letter thanks Augustine for "counselling him to form a good resolution." The counselor informs Augustine that he has also been evangelizing Volusianus: "For I have every day some discussion with the same man, so far as my abilities, or rather my lack of talent, may enable me."[45] The counselor says Augustine's letter has struck home with Volusianus, however: "On receiving this letter from your venerable Eminence, though he is kept back from firm faith in the true God by the influence of a class of persons who abound in this city, he was so moved, that, as he himself tells me, he was prevented only by the fear of undue prolixity in his letter from unfolding to you every possible difficulty in regard to the Christian faith."[46]

The difficulty Volusianus has, according to the counselor, is "that in His works the Lord performed nothing beyond what other men have been able to do. They are accustomed to bring forward their Apollonius and Apuleius, and other men who professed magical arts, whose miracles they maintained to have been greater than the Lord's."[47] This was not the nobleman's only difficulty, however. "Even if a reasonable account of the Lord's incarnation were now given to him, it would still be very difficult to give a satisfactory reason why this God, who is affirmed to be the God also of the Old Testament, is pleased with new sacrifices after having rejected the ancient sacrifices." Another concern

---

44 Ibid.
45 Letter 136.
46 Ibid.
47 Ibid.

of the nobleman is "that the Christian doctrine and preaching were in no way consistent with the duties and rights of citizens; because, to quote an instance frequently alleged, among its precepts we find, 'Recompense to no man evil for evil,' and, 'Whosoever shall smite thee on one cheek, turn to him the other also; and if any man take away thy coat, let him have thy cloak also; and whosoever shall compel thee to go a mile, go with him twain;' all which he affirms to be contrary to the duties and rights of citizens. For who would submit to have anything taken from him by an enemy, or forbear from retaliating the evils of war upon an invader who ravaged a Roman province?"[48] The counselor expects Augustine to respond with "a full, thorough, and luminous reply...Especially because, while this discussion was going on, a distinguished lord and proprietor in the region of Hippo was present, who ironically said some flattering things concerning your Holiness, and affirmed that he had been by no means satisfied when he inquired into these matters himself."[49]

Here we have insight into the daily life of Augustine, whose concern for the pagan nobleman's salvation was an important part of his ministry. We also see in this correspondence that not everyone was willing to turn to the Christian religion and that the excuses are the same as what we see in our own culture. Volusianus, "kept back from firm faith in the true God by the influence of a class of persons who abound in this city," has compiled a list of excuses for the sake of protecting his conscience from the truths of the gospel. Like Victorinus, the famous orator, this is an immanent figure with much to lose. Victorinus throws it all away for Christ. Volusianus does not.

Augustine would not dismiss Volusianus, however. He would respond by sending him what in our day would amount to a short book

48 Ibid.
49 Ibid.

of answers to his questions, with each section broken up by chapters.[50] Such commitment to someone who seems insincere and skeptical about matters of the Christian religion is a feat that only supernatural love for the person's soul could achieve. Such an attitude is consistent with what he writes elsewhere to those who engage the lost in apologetics or preaching: "These things, brethren, I would have you retain as the basis of your action and preaching with untiring gentleness: love men, while you destroy errors; take of the truth without pride; strive for the truth without cruelty. Pray for those whom you refute and convince of error."[51]

Augustine was successful in converting pagans from all backgrounds. He comments in one place that practicing astrologers would come to burn their books publicly after embracing the Christian faith. Many would later come to serve as ministers in the church.[52] But it was not just noblemen and everyday people who were caught up in paganism. "The university life of Africa was still vigorous and largely pagan."[53] Pagan and Christian tension was coming to a head in the early 400's, especially in Rome. Augustine needed a way to reach pagans outside the walls of his church. At times Augustine would engage pagans through letters. At times he is seen having personal conversations with them. But Augustine's most formidable weapon for tearing down the edifice of paganism was through his books, and especially the *City of God*.

---

50 See letter 138.
51 *Answer to Petilian*, 1.35.
52 Letter, 61.23.
53 Brown, *Augustine of Hippo*, 300.

City of God and Evangelism

In *City of God*, Augustine will take up the task of composing "a religious history of paganism." It was written over thirteen years and is "the most self-conscious book that he ever wrote."[1] Rome had fallen. Christians were being blamed. Christians themselves had been murdered, raped, and pillaged. An apologetic was needed. "I have undertaken a defense [of the city of God] against those who prefer their own gods to the Founder of this city."[2] But the book would not be merely defensive. Its potency lies in Augustine's ability to also go on the offensive, obliterating pagan infrastructures that had been in place since the time of Homer, over a thousand years earlier.

Turning the Tables on the Pagans

The pagans of Augustine's day were "fanatical antiquarians."[3] They

---

1 Brown, *Augustine of Hippo*, 302.
2 *City of God*, 1.1.
3 Brown, *Augustine of Hippo*, 303.

believed their religion alone had a pristine tradition. They were obsessed with the origin of their religion. This determined the strategy of his attack on the pagan cults.[4] But Augustine "intercepts the pagans in their last retreat to the past. He will expose the tainted origins of the cults that were most ancient…He will play upon insensibilities, and hint at the secret incredulity of the writers who preserved this past."[5] Augustine's desire is to gut the pagans from the inside out. "We must speak also of the earthly city, which, though it be mistress of the nations, is itself ruled by its lust of rule."[6]

Augustine's approach to paganism in *City of God* is to demonstrate the absurdity and inconsistency of paganism, in contrast to the viability and consistency of Christianity. Here we have an early example of what today would be called presuppositional apologetics. He never hides his belief in the integrity of Scripture. He never wavers in his position that the Christian God alone can provide a basis for truth, morality, and the purpose of life. This includes plundering truth from unbelievers for the purpose of exposing their erroneous worldview, since all truth is God's truth. Augustine says that if unbelievers "have perhaps said things that are truthful and can be conformed to our faith, we must not have fear of them, but even appropriate whatever we find useful from those who are, in a sense, their illegal possessors."[7] He goes on to give the example of Israel plundering the Egyptians' wealth before leaving Egypt for the promised land. Moreover, he realizes that only understanding and sympathetic readers will appreciate the truth of his arguments. The rest will only suppress them, since no amount of argument would be enough for those blind to the truth. It is only possible to see the universe in two ways, either as a Christian or as a

---

4 Ibid.
5 Ibid, 304.
6 *City of God*, 1.1.
7 *On Christian Doctrine*, 2.40.60.

rebel of God.[8]

City of God will work in a similar fashion.[9] Augustine uses pagan history against the pagans. He exploits the wisdom of pagan philosophy to eradicate their system of thought. Juxtaposition is the literary device that determines the structure of every book in the *City of God*.[10] Such a method has a spate of benefits. Augustine enables the reader to see the contrast of Christian and pagan beliefs, and the consequence of those beliefs. For the pagans, their beliefs lead to futility and incoherence. In contrast, the Christian's beliefs were historically consistent and ethically pure. The Christian solution "is imposed upon an elaborately constructed background of pagan answers to the same questions."[11] This provides a "a sense of richness and dramatic tension," which lends to a more readable and persuasive presentation.

Augustine shows that paganism's immorality can't be associated with any type of "true" religion. Obscene songs were sung to pagan gods.[12] The pagan gods themselves act in vile ways, killing each other, raping women, lying to get ahead. If the gods act in such bestial ways, what types of behavior could ever be condemned as evil or immoral? How could such gods ever help a city like Rome? Augustine considers such gods to be demons sent by Satan to deceive people into going to hell.[13] Such gods are not gods, but rather evil entities preying on human sinfulness. In this way the pagans are worshipping a false religion and one which can't sustain a city like Rome, since the people who follow such self-seeking gods will naturally act in the same way, destroying their commonwealth from within.

---

8 See *City of God* 2.1; 22.22, 22.24.
9 See "Augustine verses paganism" by Zachery Oliver (Dec. 21, 2014) for a helpful treatment of the following three paragraphs. Theologygaming.com. Last accessed July 22, 2021.
10 Brown, *Augustine of Hippo*, 305.
11 Ibid.
12 *City of God*, 2.4.
13 Ibid, 2.10.

Next, Augustine demonstrates the gods' ambivalence towards the happenings of Rome. This is particularly devastating since he employs history to critique the history of Rome. Romulus killed his own brother shortly after founding Rome.[14] But the Romans don't condemn the fratricide, and neither do the pagan gods. Later, Rome becomes victim to countless deaths through wars, plagues and internal conflicts—but again the pagan gods are silent.[15] It is foolish to blame Christianity for the recent destruction of Rome since this had been part of its history since its conception. Thus, paganism has neither moral nor historical foundation, and hence is unsustainable—as its history has demonstrated.

"Two City Theory" and Evangelism

It is in this context in which Augustine's "two city theory" emerges. The world has always consisted of a division between the earthly and heavenly city. The earthly city is epitomized by Cain, who was "fully rooted and at home in world."[16] By contrast, Abel was an occupant of the heavenly city, even though he also dwelt in the world. Abel longed for the things of God, aware of the transience of life in the world."[17] Abel is a "resident stranger."[18] He is persecuted and often killed by his enemy, but his hope is in God. "Cain built a city, while Abel, as though he were merely a pilgrim on earth, built none. For the true City of the saints is in heaven, though here on earth it produces citizens in whom it wanders as on a pilgrimage through time, looking for the Kingdom of eternity."[19] Augustine characterizes the two cities as being based

---

14 Ibid, 3.6.
15 Ibid, 3.31.
16 Brown, *Augustine of Hippo*, 319.
17 Ibid, 322.
18 *City of God*, 18.1, 3.
19 Ibid, 15.1.

upon two kinds of love: "Earthly society has flowered from a selfish love which dared to despise even God, whereas the heavenly is rooted in a love of God that is read to trample on self. In a word, the latter relies on the Lord, whereas the other boasts that it can get along by itself. The one seeks human glory, whereas the height of glory for the other is to hear God in the witness of the conscience…In the earthly city both the rulers themselves and the people they dominate are dominated by the lust for domination, whereas in the *City of God* all citizens serve one another in charity."[20]

This theme of the two cities battling it out on the same plane is not only found in *City of God*. Augustine develops it throughout the later part of his ministry, both in sermons and various other writings such as catechisms. In his *On Catechizing Beginners*, written for pagans interested in joining the church, Augustine writes: "The inhabitants of the earthly city who prefer their own gods to the Founder of the holy City do not realize that He is the God of gods. And so there are two cities, one of the wicked, the other of the saints, cities that existed from the beginning of the human race and so on down to the end of the ages…All those human beings who are lovers of pride and of dominating worldly things with empty vanity and flashy arrogance and all those spirits who love such things and strive for glory by subjugating people are bound together as a single society…On the other hand, all those human beings and all those spirits, all who humbly search for God's glory, and not their own, and follow along after Him in piety, also belong to a single society."[21]

Elsewhere he describes the two cities as follows: "So there's a certain godless city, described as likeminded in its human godlessness even though scattered among all the world's lands, and in the Scriptures it

---

20 Ibid, 14.28.
21 *On Catechizing Beginners*, 19.31.

is known mystically as Babylon. On the other hand, there's a certain city, on this earth a pilgrim among all the world's peoples, likeminded in godliness, and this one's called Jerusalem."[22] This idea of pilgrimage also comes up in the beginning of his homiletics book, *On Christian Doctrine*:

> Suppose, then, that we were wandering pilgrims who could not live happily except in our native land, and that we, feeling miserable from wandering and yearning to end this home-sickness, decided to go back home: we would need vehicles of some sort, to go either by land or sea, that we would use to reach our homeland, where we could find true enjoyment. But suppose we ended up enjoying the pleasures of the journey, even the delights of the vehicles themselves, getting side-tracked, enjoying what we should be using, and unwilling to finish our journey home quickly, having been ensnared in wrong-turned pleasures, and so alienating ourselves from a homeland whose savory sweetness could make us truly happy. So it is that we are 'wanderers from the Lord' on the road of this mortal life. If we wish to return to our homeland, where we can be truly happy, we must use this world, not enjoy it, in such a way that…we may grasp what is eternal and spiritual through what is bodily and temporal.[23]

In *City of God*, "Augustine had divided men into two classes according to their inner dispositions or their final destinies."[24] What is important for evangelism, however, is that these two classes of people are often indistinguishable from each other. "Now [these cities] are

---

22 Sermon 299A.8 (Dolbeau 4).
23 *On Christian Doctrine*, 1.3.3.
24 Markus, *Saeculum*, 118.

mixed together physically, in terms of bodies, but are separate in terms of wills, and on Judgment Day, will be separated in body as well."[25] "Both cities are now mixed up together; at the end they will be separated."[26] Augustine likewise points out that "God is incredibly merciful and patient with ungodly human beings and gives them opportunity for repentance and correction."[27]

Towards the end of book one, Augustine cautions the people of the city of God to "bear in mind, that among her enemies lie hid those who are destined to be fellow-citizens, that she may not think it a fruitless labor to bear what they inflict as enemies until they become confessors of the faith."[28] Christians were experiencing harassment from the invading barbarians. They had been killed and raped. Bitterness towards their enemies was an understanding reality. Augustine admonishes against it by reminding them that their enemies could end up getting converted and being part of the same city of God as themselves. Moreover, the barbarians could be converted by the Christians "bearing what they [the barbarians] inflict" in a way that honors Christ. It would be like heaping coals on the heads of their enemies. Suffering their onslaught with meekness and forgiveness could prick their conscience and turn them to the faith. Augustine notes that if this were to happen, the pain they endure would not be a "fruitless labor." Here we see the mindset of the evangelist. He is saying that as you are persecuted by the Vandals, remember that some Vandals will be saved, perhaps by your own efforts. If so, then the evils you endure would not be in vain.

In a remarkable maneuver, Augustine then reminds his Christian readers that many in their own midst will prove to be false converts,

---

25 *On Catechizing Beginners*, 19.31.
26 Sermon 299A.8 (Dolbeau 4).
27 *On Catechizing Beginners*, 19.31.
28 *City of God*, 1.35.

and hence just as bad off as the Vandals. "These men you may today see thronging the churches with us, tomorrow crowding the theatres with the godless."[29] The church has hypocrites among it. They won't belong to the eternal city, unlike some of the barbarians who are today persecuting the church but are later on converted. "Many who seem to be without [the city of God] are in reality within, and many who seem to be within yet really are without."[30] Augustine frequently draws on images and parables from the gospels to emphasize his point—the sheep and the goats, the good tree and evil tree, the wheat and the tares, the house with vessels for honor, some for dishonor. Therefore, the Christian must guard against bitterness when it comes to their enemies, but instead should use such occasions for an occasion to share the gospel.

Retreat from the World Is Condemned

Augustine's view of the heavenly city was never meant to be a prescription for flight or retreat from the world. It was not an excuse to avoid evangelizing those in the earthly city. This is important for Augustine's approach to evangelism. Augustine never assumes the Christian life should preclude engagement with the lost or even the culture in which one lives. The theme of *City of God* is "our business within this common mortal life."[31] An example of this is Augustine persuading a general not to become a monk.[32] In another place he stresses that a Christian who has the chance to serve his city as a magistrate has the duty to do so.[33] In his *Questions on the Gospels*, he foreshadows the view of the Reformers that lay Christians can "keep the wheel

---

29 Ibid, 1.35.
30 *On Baptism*, 5.38.
31 *City of God*, 15.21.15.
32 Brown, *Augustine of Hippo*, 324
33 *City of God*, 19.6.

of the world's business turning in ways that can be put to the service of God."[34] At one time, Augustine would have done differently. Not anymore. Christians must engage the world with the gospel. Christians can't entirely extricate themselves from the messiness of living in the world. Augustine's own monastery was a living embodiment of that reality. Far from being isolationists, the monastery was a training ground for ministers and church planters who would eventually supply a large number of North African churches with gospel preachers: "These too who came from that fellowship of holy men [Augustine's monastery] increased the churches of the Lord, and also established monasteries, and as their zeal for the spreading of the Word of God grew, they furnished other churches with their brethren whom they promoted to the priesthood."[35] This was an especially critical feature in North Africa due to the Church's shortage of clergy.[36] Augustine saw the monastery as a battle-school for Christ's "frontline soldiers."[37] "He was much opposed to a contemporary tendency for monks to think of themselves as having a quite separate calling apart from the Church as a whole, as they were called out of the Church rather than out of the world. He strongly felt that they should never refuse the call to serve as bishops or parish priests where that was what the Church needed them to do."[38]

This is similar to what Calvin would do in Geneva during the Reformation. Under Calvin's leadership, Geneva was "the hub of a vast missionary enterprise"[39] and "a dynamic center or nucleus from which the vital missionary energy it generated radiated out into the world

---

34 Ibid, 2.44.
35 Possidius, *Life of St. Augustine*, ch. 11.
36 Six-Means, *Augustine and Catholic Christianization*, 53.
37 Henry Chadwick, *Augustine: A Very Short Introduction* (Oxford Press, 1986), 59.
38 Ibid, 64.
39 Raymond K. Anderson, "Calvin and Missions," *Christian History*, 5 no. 4 (Fall 1986): 23.

beyond."[40] It was a "concentrated missionary effort."[41] Like Calvin, Augustine was eager to train and send ministers out to serve as missionaries and pastors, which is often overlooked because of Augustine's more favorable views of monasteries in general. It is clear the more mature Augustine saw monasteries as training camps, not bunkers.

The Legacy of the City of God

City of God is itself written as a deliberate confrontation with paganism.[42] It is this book that "demolishes with quite exceptional intellectual savagery the whole of the ancient ethical tradition."[43] It was the "pagan members of the Roman aristocracy" who provoked the writing of it. *City of God* could be seen as an evangelistic treatise to pagans and Christians alike, since some of it deals with Christians who had helped usher in the collapse of Rome by "tolerating paganism, heresy and immorality in the new Christian empire."[44] It was not just paganism which Augustine inveighed against. The hedonism of the Roman Empire was also taken down through a description very much resembling the twenty-first century West. Speaking of the glories of the Empire, they say:

> This is our concern, that every man be able to increase his wealth so as to supply his daily prodigalities...Let the people applaud not those who protect their interests, but those who provide them with pleasure...Let there be erected houses of

---

40 Philip E. Hughes, "John Calvin: Director of Missions," in *The Heritage of John Calvin*, ed. J. H. Bratt (Grand Rapids: Eerdmans, 1973), 45.
41 Robert M. Kingdom, "Calvinist Religious Aggression," in *The French Wars of Religion, How Important Were Religious Factors?*, ed. J. H. M. Salmon (Lexington, MA: D. C. Heath and Company, 1967), 6.
42 Brown, *Augustine of Hippo*, 311.
43 Ibid, 326.
44 Ibid, 336.

the largest and most ornate description: in these let there be provided the most sumptuous banquets, where every one who pleases may, by day or night, play, drink, vomit, dissipate. Let there be everywhere heard the rustling of dancers, the loud, immodest laughter of the theater; let a succession of the most cruel and the most voluptuous pleasures maintain a perpetual excitement. If such happiness is distasteful to any, let him be branded as a public enemy; and if any attempt to modify or put an end to it, let him be silenced, banished, put an end to.[45]

Paganism was dealt a partial death blow by the book, and a "new generation of politicians" were inspired by it to be "good sons of the church," men who were "no longer pagans, no longer neutral arbitrators in religious affairs."[46] To say Augustine was successful is an understatement. He becomes "the great 'seculizer' of the pagan past."[47] This may seem odd to a modern reader since paganism and secular are typically understood to be synonymous. This was not the case for Augustine's readers. Paganism was a very specialized type of religion, endowed with its own rituals, heroes, teachers, and followers. It had a stronghold on the spiritual climate of the time. The pagan gods lurked everywhere in Augustine's day. Even the house next to Augustine's baptistry was found to have had a floor covered in "medallions of the Nine Muses."[48] In *City of God*, Augustine reduces paganism "to purely human dimensions: they were only traditions laid down by men; adjusted to the needs of human society."[49] Augustine will demonstrate that even those who laid down pagan laws and ideas did not themselves believe in it. The

---

45 *City of God*, 2.20.
46 Brown, *Augustine of Hippo*, 336.
47 Ibid, 236.
48 Ibid, 266.
49 Ibid, 263.

Roman Empire specifically, founded by pagan ideals, is reduced "to the level of any other state, in order to beat out the gods from its history."[50] It was merely a lust for domination and an "overweening love of praise" that spurred on the rise of Rome: "They were, therefore, grasping for praise, open-handed with their money; honest in pursuit of wealth, they wanted to hoard glory. This is what they loved so wholeheartedly; for this they lived, for this they did not hesitate to die; all other lusts, they battened down this this overwhelming desire."[51]

The influence of paganism had forced Augustine to openly refute it. Upon the publication of *City of God*, Augustine stresses to his friends to make sure it is made available to pagans. He also stresses they not only read it, but meditate on its truths.[52] Through *City of God*, Augustine "almost single-handedly imposed a new image of Rome" upon his readers and hearers. He becomes "more than anyone else responsible for the disparagement of Rome which became the hallmark of any discussion of Roman politics in the Christian world."[53] Not until the Renaissance almost a thousand years later would "the trumpet of Rome's eternal greatness" again be taken seriously.

---

50 Ibid, 264.
51 *City of God*, 5.12.15-19.
52 See "Letter to Firmus," 1A.1-3 (Divjak).
53 Ernest L. Fortin, "St. Augustine," *History of Political Philosophy*, 176-205.

eight

Religious Coercion

Augustine's evangelism methodology comes with a black eye, however. Although Augustine dealt with non-Christians through writing, debating, and preaching, he was also in favor of state-sponsored suppression of thoughts anomalous to his own, along with the persons who espoused them.

Religious coercion would be endorsed by Augustine as early as 400 A.D., and his treatment of Donatists and Pelagians would later be used by Roman Catholics to justify the Inquisition and forced conversions. King Louis XIV's advisors would point to Augustine to justify Huguenot persecution in the early eighteenth century.[1] This does not mean Augustine would have approved of the Inquisition or Huguenot persecution. As we will see, Augustine's view of coercion came with important reservations which have often been overlooked in modern times. Nevertheless, coercion was used as a type of evangelistic method in order to see people saved.

---

1 Brown, *Religion and Society*, 325.

Development of Augustine's View on Coercion

It is imperative to recognize, according to Brown, that "Augustine's view of coercion is ambivalent. His attitude can't be made into a doctrine."[2] Augustine's age was one in which religious coercion was one of the "facts of life" for a bishop in rural Africa.[3] Augustine's approach to religious coercion evolved as he aged. At first, there is the more tolerant Augustine who advocates a mild Christianity of argument and persuasion only.[4] For example, in one of his early letters, he says the evangelization of the lost should be done through "education rather than by formal commands, by persuasion rather than by intimidation."[5] This is the pre-400 A.D. Augustine. But around 399 "a special mission had arrived in Carthage to close [pagan] temples," followed by additional orders which legislated against the "remnants of idolatry."[6] Augustine, a frequent visitor to Carthage, was influenced by the actions he saw being enforced against paganism. He would later admit as much in the *City of God*: "Officers of the Emperor Honorius…overthrew the temples and broke the images of false gods. And from that time to the present, during almost thirty years, who does not see how much the worship of the name of Christ has increased?"[7] In a letter he explains, "For originally my opinion was that no one should be coerced into the unity of Christ…But this opinion of mine was overcome…My own town, which was once wholly on the side of Donatus, was brought over to the Catholic unity by fear of the imperial edicts."[8]

---

2 Ibid, 260-261.
3 Ibid, 261.
4 Richard A. Munkelt, "Foreword" to *The Political and Social Ideas of St. Augustine* (New York, NY: Angelico Press, 2013), v.
5 Letter 22.5.
6 Brown, *Religion and Society*, 265.
7 *City of God*, 1.18.
8 Letter 93.17.

In Augustine's mind, such compulsion exposed people to true doctrine who otherwise would have been "too listless, or conceited, or sluggish, to take pains to examine Catholic truth!"[9] He says those who have been converted to the true faith are thankful they were coerced into attending the teachings of the Christian church: "Others say: 'We did not know that truth was here, and we did not want to learn it; but fear has made us alert to recognize it, the fear of being struck with the possible loss of temporal goods without any gain of eternal goods.' Others say: 'We were held back from entering the Church by false rumors which we could not know as false without entering, nor would we enter without being forced…' Others say: 'We thought it made no difference where we held the faith of Christ, but thanks be to the Lord who has gathered us out of our separation, and has shown us that it befits one God that men should dwell in unity.'"[10] Elsewhere in the same letter Augustine claims those who have been coerced into the church, upon believing the gospel, agree it was his duty to act in the manner which he did: "How many of them, now rejoicing with us, speak bitterly of the weight with which their ruinous course formerly oppressed them, and confess that it was our duty to inflict annoyance upon them, in order to prevent them from perishing under the disease of lethargic habit, as under a fatal sleep."[11]

Around this time, one of Augustine's sermons includes a defense of the public coercion of a leading pagan by comparing it to "the forcible conversion of Paul, who had also been converted *ex necessitate*."[12] He would use such ideas extensively after 405 to justify religious coercion. Augustine's first official work against the Donatists came in 400, in

---

9 Ibid.
10 Letter 93.18.
11 Ibid, 93.
12 Brown, *Religion and Society*, 266.

which half his attitude to coercion is already fully developed.[13] The Christian Emperor had a right "to punish, restrain and repress, those impious cults over which God's providence had given them dominion."[14]

The other half of his attitude was defined along theological lines. We have already seen how Augustine's optimism about the expansion of the church influenced his outlook of evangelism in his younger years, and the same could be said about religious coercion. Augustine's defense of coercion was largely dependent upon the belief that the Church should be diffused among all nations.[15] If this was certain, it made sense that pagans, Jews and heretics should be repressed throughout the Roman Empire. Much of his "heady optimism" was the direct result of Christian victory over paganism in Rome in the century preceding Augustine's. Despite the increasing encroachment of the barbarians, it did not look like Christian conquest would diminish any time soon.[16] Augustine's vision of the fulfillment of prophecy in history—that the Church should prevail among all the nations—led to the conclusion that such punishment could be coercive in the full sense of the word.[17]

The large number of pagans who converted to Christianity only fanned the flame. Augustine, by nature "a peace-loving man, intensely sensitive to violence," becomes swept up by the opportunity to create a Christian world in the literal sense of that term. This point is somewhat clouded by the fact that Augustine would suppress Pelagians in a similar manner later in life, after Rome falls and Christianity becomes exposed to ridicule, but the foundation of his theory was intertwined

---

13 Ibid.
14 Ibid.
15 Ibid.
16 Ibid, 267.
17 Ibid, 268.

with a particular view of eschatology that gave momentum and even justification for squashing dissenters.

Predestination and Coercion

Between 403 and 405, Augustine frequently states he had been unwilling to impose such full coercive measure against the Donatists.[18] It would change within a matter of years. What was the reason? There had been a concern among church leaders about feigned conversions.[19] His own church had been victim to a low spiritual state due to large amounts of pagans coming in when Christianity became an official religion. For this reason, adding more people to the church who weren't genuinely Christian seemed counterproductive. Most ministers in our own context would agree. "Augustine's early letters and sermons on the rowdy celebrations of the Parentalia in Africa…show how he regarded the low standards of his own congregation as having arisen, largely, from 'hypocrisy,'" or false professors. This is what kept him from subscribing to full coercion. What is the church supposed to do with a hoard of false professors? What would be the benefit?

Augustine's reluctance changed, however, when he began to view the situation through the lens of grace and predestination. This is particularly important for how we deal with Augustine's evangelism methodology. Augustine was confident the Church could not only absorb false professors through religious coercion, but that such false professors could be genuinely converted through the process. To object to religious coercion "because it produced such feigned conversions came to appear as tantamount to denying 'the Power of God,' Who could seek out His own among the multitude who had conformed

---

18 Ibid.
19 Ibid.

with a bad grace to the Catholic Church."[20] Such a view appears to be a type of evangelistic pragmatism. Since the goal of conversion may be achieved by religious coercion, religious coercion becomes a viable option. God can use such coercion to bring more people into the true Church, and hence, more people will be exposed to the way of salvation. God's grace could work a change of heart even in men who had been forced into the Catholic Church. The problem of "feigned conversions" becomes God's, not man's, since only God knows the heart of the man.

This is demonstrated in Augustine's response to the conversion of a banker named Faustinus. Locals assumed he was feigning conversion in order to be nominated mayor, a position closed off to non-Christians. In a sermon preached in Carthage, home to Faustinus, Augustine appeals to his hearers to give Faustinus the benefit of the doubt. He rebukes his hearers for casting doubt on the work of God. "One who used to be an enemy of the Christian faith, has now embraced the Christian faith. Some may say: 'Who? That guy, a Christian? That guy, he has come to believe?'…You cannot peer into the heart of new Christians…You're going to say, 'But Faustinus believed because he had to.' The same could be said of the one I talked about a little earlier. St. Paul, too, at one point was 'a blasphemer and a persecutor and a scoffer.' He also got forced, a certain necessity imposed on him. A heavenly voice laid him flat."[21] Not stopping there, Augustine next exhorts his hearers to take Faustinus in and teach him the way of Christianity. "Love him abundantly in all his doubting. By your love, remove doubts from the heart of one who is less than firm…People will say, 'Who used to be against Christ?' 'Faustinus.' 'Who now fears Christ?' 'Faustinus.'…And so, brothers, we commend him to your prayers, and to your love, and to a most faithful friendship, and to holding him up when he's less than

---

20 Ibid, 269.
21 Sermon 279.10.

firm. As you move along, teach him the good pathway. Let him find that good pathway in you. Now that he's been made a Christian, let him discern the difference between what he has dismissed and what he has found."[22] Augustine concludes, "Faustinus got minted by Christ as a brand-new banker…Rejoice, exult, love him—more than you ever despised him."[23]

Previously, the tradition within Christianity was to view freedom of choice as an important element for healthy and true religion. "A religious institution which resorted to force must be a merely human artifice."[24] But Augustine would answer: "If I were propose to you the question how God the Father draws men to the Son, when He has left them to themselves in freedom of action, you would perhaps find it difficult of solution. For how does He draw them to Him if He leaves them to themselves, so that each should choose as he pleases?"[25] Augustine's view of man is important here. Man is enslaved to his own lusts, and hence, his freedom can never lead him to the truth since he has no desire for it. But if that same man is forced to be exposed to the truth, God can use it to convert such a man. Some of his critics expressed shock by Augustine's proposal to use the state to coerce or discipline spiritual opponents. Augustine believed, however, fallen man "required more than purely spiritual pressures to keep him from evil."[26]

For Augustine, the decision of a person's will is always preceded by a long process, among other things, "of fear, of constraint, of external inconveniences." Most of the time the person is unaware of such factors, but they are influential on a person's decisions. This led to what Brown calls "one of his most profound and original contributions to

---

22 Ibid, 279.11.
23 Ibid, 279.12.
24 Brown, *Religion and Society*, 269.
25 Ibid, 270.
26 Brown, *Augustine of Hippo*, 368.

ethical thought."[27] Augustine recognizes "external impingements" are a large factor in moral development. Examples of this would include fear of death and the inconveniences of the life of the senses. Such fears and inconveniences influence us in healthy ways. Therefore "a coercive policy, in imposing a series of direct physical restraints and penalties on the individual, would seem to lead to a sudden debasement of motives."[28] A person would become more persuaded to do the right thing even if it did not entail a supernatural heart change—but over time, it could lead to a supernatural heart change. Those who come over due to fear or self-interest could acquire in time a genuine conviction of the truth. Augustine would find examples from the Old Testament to justify his outlook: "The profoundly meaningful institutions of Israel had been imposed on the majority of Israelites frankly by fear; the Law was a *paedagogus*—it had acted, coercively, by threats."[29] Thus, fear can be a legitimate element in both enforcing a religious establishment and convicting people of the true faith.

Coercion - How Far Should It Go?

Coercion was not to be a means of torture and execution. Augustine's approach to coercion was tempered by his view of it being a disciplining process of the church. "His usual term for 'coercion' is not *cohercitio*—root of our own word—which had retained its purely negative, legal meaning of 'restraint' and 'punishment': it is *correptio*—'rebuke'—defined by its aim, *correctio*, 'setting right.'"[30] It was not to be purely punitive, but a positive process of corrective treatment that was meant to lead to the person's spiritual and even physical good, not harm. It

27 Brown, *Religion and Society*, 271.
28 Ibid.
29 Sermon 62, 8.
30 Brown, *Religion and Society*, 274.

was to be a "treatment by inconveniencies," not mutilation.[31]

Because Augustine had thought so much about the issue, he was able to act rationally and even with sympathy towards dissenters. He would gladly welcome false professors into his church. He was willing to work with them. He genuinely believed they could be saved by the power of the gospel. "Augustine lived in a violent and authoritarian age. The death penalty and brutal tortures were indiscriminately imposed. At least it can be said of Augustine that he kept his head."[32] His own words provide a glimpse of his conscious responsibility when it came to coercion: "What shall I say as to the infliction and remission of punishment in cases in which we only desire to forward the spiritual welfare of those we are deciding whether or not to punish?... What trembling we feel in these things…What a darkness!...O that I had wings like a dove, for then I should fly away and be at rest."[33] He admits in this same letter, "I confess that I make mistakes daily in regard to this."[34] Another historian claims, "Until the very end of his life, the church leader endorsed only mild penalties of an external nature for religious insurgency, such as fines or confiscation of property, rather than corporeal punishments such as torture, mutilation, or the death penalty."[35] This can be seen when he discovers that Victorinus had been posing as a Christian deacon in order to work behind the scenes as a Manichean evangelist. Augustine claims, "I was horrified at his duplicity under his clerical guise," something any minister could relate to. Augustine responds by taking steps "to have him confined and driven from the city."[36] He then notifies other ministers to the deceit of Victorinus, but nowhere is Augustine seen pushing for the

---

31 Brown, *Augustine of Hippo*, 305.
32 Brown, *Religion and Society*, 276.
33 *Nicene and Post-Nicene Fathers*, Letter, 204, 2.
34 Letter, 204.2.
35 Munkelt, "Foreword" to *The Political and Social Ideas of St. Augustine*, vi.
36 Letter, 236.3.

man's death or torture, which would have been normal enough in his environment.

Augustine's "two city theory" has often led to the accusation of Augustine advocating withdrawal and pacifism, even in his own day.[37] But Augustine, like his contemporaries, "knew what it was to wield power with the support of the Imperial administration."[38] When dealing with heresy he had shown not a trace of pacifism.[39] Augustine believed laws "revealed to men by divine authority and actively enforced, were to be the basis of his Christian empire."[40] When comparing Augustine to one of his theological enemies, Julian of Eclanum, Brown notes that whereas Julian's side of the Mediterranean boasted of "hospitality, wise words, fair judgment," for Augustine's Africa, their churches were inscribed with "fighting-slogans."[41] In this regard Augustine is a man of his times and culture. "He will argue in favor of suppressing heresy from the dangerous analogy of social restraints on all levels."[42] Augustine writes to heretics that "Christian rulers should, rather, impose on such men as you are, fitting discipline and punishment."[43]

Coercion and Evangelism

But there is an aspect of Augustine's view that is novel and of much relevance for the purposes of evangelism. What was Augustine's motive for suppression? Was it coldness or even hatred for his opponents? Was it fear of his opponents' views? Was it blind agreement to partake in an action that was popular in his time, unaware of its devastating

---

37 Brown, *Augustine of Hippo*, 283.
38 Ibid, 289-290.
39 Ibid, 290.
40 Ibid.
41 Ibid, 384.
42 Ibid, 392.
43 Ibid, 364.

consequences for the future? Strangely enough, he seemed to be doing it out of genuine concern for his opponents. If his opponents were to receive the truth, "it can be done with greater ease, in my opinion, when the teaching of truth is aided by the fear of severity."[44] Augustine wrote the only full justification in the history of the Early Church of the right of the state to suppress non-Catholics,[45] but it should be seen as much as possible without the baggage of later Inquisitions. Such actions would be a far cry from Augustine's desires. For Augustine, religious coercion remained a genuinely corrective treatment.[46] He sought to win over hardened rivals, not stamp out a small minority.[47] He wanted coercion done with tact: "For if they were only being terrorized, and not instructed at the same time, this would be an inexcusable tyranny on our part."[48] In another letter he explains his policy in greater detail: "We desire their repentance, not their death, in order that they may be saved from falling into the penalties of the eternal judgment. We do not wish to see them quite absolved from punishment nor, on the other hand, visited with the torments which they deserve. Check their sins, therefore, in such a way as to produce repentance in at least a few."[49]

It is difficult to be sympathetic to Augustine's position in light of what would happen later on in church history. But Augustine was consistent in his attitude to correct his opponent with truth, not crush or destroy them physically. "A bishop named Consentius asked Augustine if he would approve the use of *agents provocateurs* 'to obtain the names of heretics in his church.'" Augustine responded with fury to this "ingenious hunting with lies." Rather, he said, "it would be easier for their error to be uprooted by truthful arguments, and it is up to you

---

44 *Nicene and Post-Nicene Fathers*, Letter 191, 2.
45 Brown, *Augustine of Hippo*, 231.
46 Ibid, 236.
47 Ibid.
48 *Nicene and Post-Nicene Fathers*, Letter 93, ii, 3.
49 Letter, 100.1.

to get down to writing these."[50]

On some occasions, Augustine would plead for the lives of his enemies to be spared by the civil magistrate. In 412, for example, Donatists attacked two Christian clergy, killing one and dismembering the other. The Donatists were convicted of the crime but Augustine wrote to the imperial judge, a Christian, asking him to commute the death sentence against them.[51] "When I heard that they had confessed to these crimes, I had not the slightest doubt that they would be subject to capital punishment at your hands. So I have made haste to write this letter to your Nobility, begging and praying for you, by the mercy of Christ...not to allow similar tortures to be inflicted on them...I am at ease about the men who have confessed, that they will not suffer reciprocal treatment...As a bishop I warn a Christian, and as a Christian I appeal to a judge, not to let this happen."[52] Augustine provides his reasons later in the letter: "If no lesser punishment were possible for them, we should prefer to let them go free, rather than avenge the martyrdom of our brothers by shedding their blood...Strive to outdo the wickedness with goodness. By a monstrous crime they tore limbs from a living body; you can, by a work of mercy, make them apply to some useful work the wholly intact limbs that they exercised in their unspeakable deeds. They did not spare the servants of God who were preaching repentance to them. Spare them now that you have arrested, summoned, and convicted them. They shed Christian bloods with impious sword. Withhold, for Christ's sake, even the sword of the law for their blood...It befits you, a Christian judge, in a case involving the church, to be such as this; for this we beg, we urge, we intervene. People tend to appeal against sentences deemed too light, but we so love our

---

50 Brown, *Augustine of Hippo*, 236.
51 As found in *Augustine In His Own Words*, Ed. by William Harmless (Washington D.C.: Catholic University Press, 2010), 97-100.
52 Letter 134.1-4.

enemies that we would appeal this severe sentence to you—if we did not rely on your Christian obedience."[53] Such consistency is further shown when "Augustine would visit jails to protect prisoners from ill-treatment: he would intervene, tactfully but firmly, to save criminals from judicial torture and execution."[54] He would oftentimes arbitrate in their lawsuits.[55]

Tension with the Donatists

Augustine's opponents used tactics as suppressive as his, and often more violent.[56] Augustine believed "corrective treatment fails in its purpose, if it exterminates the subject.[57] In contrast, a Donatist bishop, upon his return to Hippo after a political upheaval put the Donatists back into power, spoke of Augustine as a marked man, "a wolf, to be slain."[58] Augustine was "faced with the prospect of ending his life as a martyr. Only the mistake of a guide in choosing the wrong road saved him from ambush."[59]

On Augustine's side, he seems more comfortable with literary or even public debates. Possidius relates, "He even wrote private letters to prominent bishops of this error [of Donatism] and to laymen, urging and exhorting them by the arguments which he offered that they should either abandon the error or at least enter into a discussion with him. In their distrust they were never willing even to answer him in writing, but in anger spoke furiously, privately and publicly declaring that Augustine was a seducer and deceiver of souls. They said and

---

53 Ibid.
54 Brown, *Augustine of Hippo*, 189.
55 Ibid.
56 Ibid, 288.
57 Ibid, 293.
58 Ibid, 330.
59 Ibid.

preached that the wolf must be killed in defense of their flock, and neither fearing God nor ashamed before men, they taught the people to believe that whoever should be able to do this would undoubtedly have all his sins forgiven of God. Meanwhile Augustine sought to make known to all their lack of confidence in their own cause, and when they met in public conferences they did not dare to debate with him."[60]

A local conference made up of Donatists and Catholics marks the intensity of their rivalry, and thus provides a window into Augustine's times. "Both sides stood around on a hot summer's afternoon, as each Donatist bishop recognized his Catholic rival. Tempers soon became frayed. Memories of violence broke into the monotony of the roll-call. 'Here I am. Put it down. Does Florentius recognize me? He should. He put me in prison for four years, and would have had me executed...' 'I recognize my persecutor...' By now the lights are lit. A single incident threatens to steer the whole proceedings into a cul de sac: had the Donatists signed on behalf of a dead bishop? 'It is only human to die,' Petilian had said. 'It may be human for a man to die,' Alypius snapped back: 'but it is unworthy of a man to lie.'"[61] These were common scenes in Augustine's day. It is not "class, race or education" that provokes Augustine's actions, but rather "the watershed of ideas and highly personal assumption."[62] And it existed on both sides, as we have seen. Donatists were often guilty of destroying Catholic altars and "purifying" their basilicas with whitewash. They carried clubs called "Israel's" which they used to demolish anything idolatrous, crying out as they did so, "Praise to God!" "The list of Catholic clergy who suffered maiming, or blinding when lime and vinegar were thrown into their eyes, or outright death, was not short."[63] It was said both churches by that time

---

60 Possidius, *Life of St. Augustine*, Ch. 9.
61 Brown, *Augustine of Hippo*, 333.
62 Ibid, 212.
63 Chadwick, *Augustine: A Very Short Introduction*, 81.

had a record of violence,[64] but the Donatists' more extreme sect—the Circumcellions—were nothing short of monstrous. It was reported of a Catholic bishop named Maximinian that Donatists smashed an altar over his head, slashed his groin with a machete, and then threw him off a tower onto a bed of ash. Somehow he survived, travelling to Ravenna to show his scars to the emperor and to plead for stricter measures against the Donatists.[65]

Conclusion

Despite our modern distaste for anything that smacks of coercion, and rightfully so, it can't be denied Augustine's motive was a desire to see his opponents come to a knowledge of the truth. His methods were primitive and grim compared to our standards, but for a man of Augustine's time, who had the civil authorities at his disposal, this is what we should expect from someone eager to see people saved. It was also perfectly normal to use the state to coerce the lost, as is seen from Constantine's reign in the 320's all the way into Augustine's day. Constantine specifically had issued edicts against "Arius, wicked and impious," and that "whoever hides them shall be condemned to death."[66] Constantine also prescribed the burning of Arian tracts and other measures to coerce dissenting religious groups. In 382 A.D. another law is issued imposing the death penalty for anyone who celebrates Easter on the wrong day of the year. In Rome in 407 a decree was made that "if any images stand even now in the temples and shrines…they shall be torn from their foundations…Altars shall be destroyed in all places."[67]

Augustine understood the Christian "must coexist with sinners in

---

64 Brown, *Augustine of Hippo*, 225.
65 Chadwick, *Augustine of Hippo: A Life*, 110-111.
66 MacMullen, *Christianizing the Roman Empire*, 93.
67 Ibid, 101.

the same community as himself, a task involving humility and integrity. But he must also be prepared, actively, to rebuke and correct them."[68] This is a type of open confrontation with the lost. This is Augustine's mindset when it comes to using the state to suppress heresy. In Augustine's mind, if the state is at the disposal of Christians, able to be used for the sake of enforcing Christian truth, suppressing dissension, and converting unbelievers, why not use it? Why let such an opportunity be wasted?

Augustine's evangelistic pragmatism as it relates to coercion is disappointing. Thankfully, we as modern Christians can't typically relate to using coercion as a means to grow a religion. Augustine demonstrates here that he is man of clay, prone to blind spots and poor decisions that we a thousand years later can more accurately assess. He also demonstrates that the line between peaceful coercion and that which is more violent is often a simple one to cross. Around the beginning of the fifth century, Augustine flies into a reverie against paganism, crying out "that all superstition of pagans and heathens should be annihilated is what God wants, God commands, God proclaims!" Such words elicited wild applause, and at least a couple biographers have suggested it also led to religious riots which left sixty people dead.[69]

But we must also admit that Augustine seems to have chosen such a route for the benefit of his neighbor, not their harm. It would also be fair to say that he would disapprove of the type of violence and execution of the type later used by the Roman Catholic Church. Augustine was perhaps guilty of laying the groundwork for such measures and for stirring up others to go too far in their crusade against non-Christians, but to say he was culpable for later evils in the church seems hyperbolic.

---

68 Brown, *Augustine of Hippo*, 218.
69 MacMullen, *Christianizing the Roman Empire*, 95; Meer (1961), 39 and Brown (1972), 308.

It is fairer to say that Augustine had failed to see the consequences of his view and even his rhetoric. The lesson here is to stick to the biblical means of evangelism, regardless of how "effective" another approach might seem. Had Augustine done so, such a chapter in his life—and this book—would likely never have come up.

Miracles and Pragmatism

Perhaps the most concerning influence on Augustine's evangelism is what has been called the "charismatic perspective."[1] Later in life, Augustine would resort to miracles and relics to substantiate his theological arguments and appeal to the people. This chapter is not an endorsement of such views. It is a recognition of the complexity of Augustine's evangelism methodology, especially as it relates to the culture in which he lived.

Such a charismatic perspective "played on all significant actions" in the times of Augustine. Visions would guide the emperor Constantine into victory and the notorious Saint Antony into the desert. "Dreams commanding baptism, for instance, was a common feature of popular Christianity in the ancient world."[2] Augustine is thrilled to report that Ambrose was instructed in a dream where to find the remains of martyred Christians.[3] In the same place he speaks of a woman of Carthage

---

1 Brown, *Augustine of Hippo*, 507.
2 Ibid, 416.
3 *City of God*, 22.8.

whose cancer was cured after she received a dream instructing her about a miracle remedy. In his *Confessions* he relates several instances of his mother receiving dreams and revelations directly from God, one of which directly foretelling his conversion to Christianity.

This can be uncomfortable for Christians in the West who are typically bereft of such experiences. Augustine himself once shared such sympathies. He "had once mocked Donatist claims based on such revelations."[4] He thought it unseemly and ludicrous to use such arguments as miracles in theological discussion. By the end of his ministry, however, he came to embrace miracles both in everyday life and to assert the validity of his theological arguments. As his popularity mounted, he even had the experience of realizing he himself had played a role in the dreams of many people. "On his deathbed, a sick man was brought to Augustine to be healed. His first reaction was to joke: 'If I had the gift you say, I would be the first to try it on myself; but, as soon as heard that the man had been told to come to him by a dream, he laid his hands on him."[5]

Miracles and Evangelism

What does this have to do with evangelism? Miracles and the relics associated with them became a prominent feature in drawing large crowds of people to a certain place where Augustine could then address them in a sermon. They were also an important apologetic tool against pagans and other non-believers. This was nothing new in Christian circles of the time. Historian Ramsay MacMullen has even noted miracles were the greatest weapon for converting pagans to Christi-

---

4 Brown, *Augustine of Hippo*, 416.
5 *Vita*, XXIX, 5.

anity.[6] He notes instances such as lost items being found by holy men, people raised from the dead, crop-destroying demons being dispelled, temples overthrown by prayer alone, and other examples which led to people's conversion to Christianity.[7] Other examples include exorcisms and healings of the mind and body at certain shrines.[8] Augustine had once "spoken scathingly of such popular beliefs," but eventually "he found himself preaching to huge crowds" drawn by them.[9] Augustine's colleagues likewise "made use of these new relics" to strengthen their hand with the populace.[10] A sudden wave of miraculous cures became associated with the relics, with "seventy taking place in Hippo within the space of two years."[11]

Such an evangelistic motive explains the tension in Augustine's thought pertaining to miracles. In 390, as a younger man, he posited "miracles such as had happened in the times of the Apostles were no longer allowed to take place."[12] He encouraged the faithful to look to nature to see the miraculous. "The daily miracles of creation are as great as those of the incarnate Lord." The sun rising each morning, the seasons changing in a regular pattern each year, trees sprouting forth from seeds the size of pebbles, babies growing inside of their mothers, the flight of birds in the sky—each in their own way are dazzling displays of the power and wisdom of God. In another place he claims the miracle of conversion is greater than the material miracles done by Christ himself while on earth. The Lord opens blind hearts now, not

---

6 Ramsay MacMullen, *Christianizing the Roman Empire* (New Haven, CT: Yale University, 1984), 62-63.
7 Ramsay MacMullen, *Christianity & Paganism in the Fourth to Eighth Centuries* (New Haven, CT: Yale University, 1997), 9.
8 MacMullen, *Christianity & Paganism in the Fourth to Eighth Centuries*, 11.
9 Brown, *Augustine of Hippo*, 417.
10 Ibid.
11 Ibid.
12 Ibid, 419.

just eyes.[13] This being the case, what other miracles would a person need to have?

Yet even then Augustine is seen witnessing and accepting "cures associated with the spectacular discovery of the bodies" of Christian martyrs in Milan. Thus, in his riper years, when he seems to give way to the apparent reality of miracles associated with dreams and relics, it can't be seen as acquiescence to something altogether foreign to his thinking. It is not a submission to a thing he does not believe in for the sake of achieving some end. It was not insincere. "Rather, within the immensely complex structure of Augustine's thought, the center of gravity had shifted; modern miracles, which had once been peripheral, now become urgently important as supports of the faith."[14]

Henry Chadwick has documented the shift in Augustine's thinking as taking place sometime after 404. Augustine writes to Paulinus of Nola with puzzlement that "in Africa, despite its many shrines," such wonders as Paulinus described happening in his area did not happen. Miracles were more or less unheard of in Hippo. The rival Donatists also claimed miracles were taking place among their people. Chadwick notes "the Catholic community might find it hard to allow their schismatic rivals to trump them." By 410 Augustine is claiming that "cures by the merit of the martyrs are becoming more frequent now."[15] Chadwick's explanation seems to cast doubt on the legitimacy of what Augustine was seeing, attributing it instead to the need to keep up with his rivals. Whatever the motive, by the end of his life Augustine is no longer hesitant to claim the veracity of miracles. In fact, he argues for them with relish in both his formal writings and letters.

Another way to look at it is to think of the younger Augustine as

---

13 Chadwick, *Augustine of Hippo: A Life*, 77.
14 Brown, *Augustine of Hippo*, 419.
15 Chadwick, *Augustine of Hippo*, 78.

the philosopher who would explain away all assumptions that seemed to imperil logic and sound argument. He was also influenced by the rationalistic tendencies that permeated his circles in Rome and Milan. In his old age, Augustine becomes jaded by the assumed wisdom of the intelligentsia and hence is more easily able to believe in the unexplainable. It also helped that he left Milan for the comparative backwaters of Hippo. For Augustine, a miracle "was just such a reminder of the bounds imposed on the mind by habit…The wise men of the ancient world had failed to map out the whole world of nature.""[16] Ancient physics and even logic could not always account for the phenomena of events that happen all the time for those who are aware of how to look for them.[17] As an old man, "he had defended with passion and conviction doctrines that ran contrary to all habitual habits of reasoning."[18] As a young man, in contrast, "he had considered that men no longer needed such spectacular proofs of their faith," even though in the early church he would grant that it was necessary.[19] As an old man, "Augustine is less sure: the human race had remained much the same, always frail, always in need of compelling authority" such as miracles.[20] It becomes apparent when reading Augustine's descriptions of miracles in his later years that he casts no doubt as to their legitimacy. They are as real as any concrete phenomena such as trees or the sun. He has an air of unquestioning certainty.

Miracles in the City of God

Augustine's *City of God* has a chapter on miracles entitled, "Of miracles which were wrought that the world might believe in Christ, and which

---

16 Brown, Augustine of Hippo, 420.
17 Ibid, 415-420.
18 Ibid, 420.
19 Ibid, 421.
20 *City of God*, 22.9 (martyred bodies have healing powers).

have not ceased since the world believed."[21] Augustine documents several miracles he has either seen or heard testimony of from individuals. In Milan there was a blind man healed while Augustine and his friend had been there as laymen. About another miracle seen by his own eyes he reports, "Yet who knows of this miracle? We know it, and so too do the small number of brethren who were in the neighborhood." Augustine speaks of a comedian of Curubis "cured at baptism not only of paralysis, but also of hernia, and being delivered of both afflictions, came up…as if he had nothing wrong with his body." He speaks of the bones of Stephen curing and converting people before his eyes. "Were I to record the miracles of healing which were wrought in the district by means of Stephen, they would fill many volumes."

Reading such a chapter through the lens of a Reformed hermeneutic can be somewhat of a roller-coaster. On the one hand, some accounts seem plausible enough. A man named Innocentius was cured of a critical stomach illness the morning after he engaged in vehement prayer: "He cast himself down, as if some one were hurling him violently to the earth, and began to pray; but in what manner, what earnestness and emotion, with what a flood of tears, with what groans and sobs, that shook his whole body…Who can describe it!" Augustine had been present during this prayer, saying to himself, "O Lord, what prayers of Thy people dost Thou hear if Thou hearest not these?" The man was discovered to be healed of his ailment the next day. Such a miracle is unproblematic. God heals people through prayers. Augustine observes in the same chapter that he knows a bishop "who once prayed for a demoniac young man whom he never saw, and that was cured on the spot." Another account has a young man praying for his father-in-law to be converted or in Augustine's words, to "believe in

---

21 Ibid, 22.8.

Christ." That night the man "declared that he believed, and he was baptized."[22] None of these events would grate against the historical Reformed view of miracles.

Other accounts are clearly problematic, however. Augustine gives credit to a memorial shrine called "Twenty Martyrs" for helping a poor man find a gold ring in a fish's belly, by means of which he was able to obtain clothes. Elsewhere, Augustine speaks of dirt brought to him from Jerusalem from the spot where Christ had been buried, over which Augustine erected a shrine. In time it became a place of prayer. "A young clergyman who was paralytic, who when he heard of this, begged his parents to take him without delay to that holy place. When he had been brought there, he prayed, and forthwith went away on his own feet perfectly cured."[23]

Augustine's involvement with miracles and relics should not be seen as any kind of subterfuge on his part. He was not a contemporary televangelist. Augustine seems to sincerely believe in the miraculous events taking place around him and on several occasions is seen energetically systemizing each account for the benefit of the public. He wished to "bend" the "shocking hardness of the reasonable pagans by a direct appeal to the astonishing things happening in the Christian communities all around them."[24] Also, miracles by themselves aren't enough to produce faith. In fact, without faith, a person won't believe the miracle. Moreover, a person is not required to see a miracle in order to have faith. Most people don't and still believe: "How is it that in enlightened times, in which every impossibility is rejected, the world has, without any miracles, believed things marvelously incredible?" Augustine even implies that miracles are for the more immature be-

---

22 Ibid.
23 Ibid.
24 Brown, *Augustine of Hippo*, 418.

liever, not the mature.

A case study of this comes from a letter Augustine wrote to "the Aged Alypius," in which he reports of a man named Dioscorus who was converted under quite marvelous circumstances. Augustine remarks that the man had a stubborn neck and bold tongue and "could not be subdued without some miracle." When his daughter was struck with illness, he vowed he would become a Christian if he saw her restored to health. Upon her recovery, he backed out of his oath, but the Lord smote him with blindness. He vowed again that if he regained his sight, he would perform what he initially vowed—that he would become a Christian. However, even after his vow, "the hand of God was still stretched forth," and the next part of Augustine's letter is perhaps the most unusual:

> He had not committed the Creed to memory, or perhaps had refused to commit it, and had excused himself on the plea of inability. God had seen this. Immediately after all the ceremonies of his reception he is seized with paralysis, affecting many, indeed almost all his members, and even his tongue. Then, being warned by a dream, he confesses in writing that it had been told to him that this had happened because he had not repeated the Creed. After that confession the use of all his members was restored to him, except the tongue alone; nevertheless he, being still under this affliction, made manifest by writing that he had, notwithstanding, learned the Creed, and still retained it in his memory; and so that frivolous loquacity which, as you know, blemished his natural kindliness, and made him, when he mocked Christians, exceedingly profane, was altogether destroyed in him. What shall I say, but, "Let us sing a hymn to the

Lord, and highly exalt Him for ever!²⁵

Such vows are also taken by non-Christians whose crops were suffering from drought, others who needed a safe voyage on the waters, and a young mother in the midst of a difficult birth. This last example was a vow taken by the woman's entire family, who said that if the woman and baby were spared from death, they would all join the church.²⁶

Pragmatism

The implications for this as they pertain to evangelism are subtle but important. We must lament Augustine's view of relics in light of biblical teaching and the tragic implications it would have in the development of Roman Catholic doctrine. We must question many of his accounts of the miracles which he describes. But through such a view Augustine gained sympathy with the populace, with the monks, and even with non-Christian groups who likewise regarded the miraculous as valid. Many will flock to Hippo for this reason. Augustine will encourage people to document their miraculous encounters and publish them to the world, not for popularity, but to convince the naysayers of the truth of Christianity. Augustine was not content to let the miraculous be kept out of sight, for the Christian's benefit only. Ever the evangelist, he would seek for ways to turn such things outward, as weapons to win people to Christ and defend the true faith against skeptics. Although the author is not in support of Augustine's conclusions regarding the miraculous, it can't be denied that Augustine, as a man of his time, sought to use what he considered to be legitimate demonstrations of

---

25 Letter 227.
26 MacMullen, *Christianizing the Roman Empire*, 87-88.

God for the sake of saving others.

That said, Augustine's pragmatism as it relates to the miraculous and evangelism is very concerning. Given Augustine's staunch belief in predestination, it is inexcusable to rely on anything for the conversion of the lost other than God's prescribed means—gospel proclamation and prayer, along with a life consistent with the gospel we proclaim. Anything other than this puts a reliance on ourselves, not God. Perhaps Augustine would argue that because God is the author of the miracle, it is perfectly acceptable to use the miraculous as a means to convert the lost. But this is inconsistent with biblical teaching, which shows that unbelievers suppress the truth in unrighteousness, and even if they saw a miracle take place before their eyes—as many did in the days of Jesus—they still wouldn't believe the gospel. Unbelievers would try to explain it away or deny it was done by God. True enough, in the early church signs and wonders were performed to validate the message of Jesus and the apostles, but the miracles in themselves were never enough to cause a lost person to believe. Besides, even false teachers and demons can perform miracles. Even in Augustine's day his spiritual opponents were claiming miracles very similar to those witnessed by Augustine. Hence the need for gospel proclamation and prayer, along with a consistently biblical lifestyle.

Conclusion

Despite Augustine's mammoth achievements and insight, we see again he was a man of his times and, as he himself would admit, far from perfect. We also see the temptation to use pragmatism for the sake of saving the lost, even if it doesn't comport with biblical teaching. While there is nothing wrong in itself about being creative in our evangelism methodologies, we must be guided by the Scriptures in everything we do. We must trust that gospel proclamation, prayer, and a life consistent with Christian teaching is enough to convert the lost and build the church. The gospel is "the power of God unto salvation for everyone who believes" (Rom. 1:16). This is why any approach to evangelism that makes the gospel secondary is unbiblical, even if it it something such as miracles.

When it comes to evangelism and specifically how people are converted, the Bible teaches it happens by people encountering the gospel. Writing to the Romans, Paul says, "So then faith comes by hearing, and hearing by the word of God" (Rom. 10:17). When writing to the Thessalonians he says, "For this reason we also thank God without ceasing, because when you received the word of God which you heard from us, you welcomed it not as the word of men, but as it is in truth, the word of God, which also effectively works in you who believe" (1 Thess. 2:13). And again, when writing to the Galatians, Paul says, "Did you receive the Spirit by the works of the Law, or by hearing with faith" (Gal. 3:2)? To the Ephesians he says, "In Him you also trusted, after you heard the word of truth, the gospel of your salvation" (Eph. 1:13). This is where biblical evangelism comes in: "How then shall they call on Him in whom they have not believed? And how shall they believe in Him of whom they have not heard? And how shall they hear without a preacher?" (Rom. 10:14). John Owen said, "The way principally insisted on by the apostles was, by preaching the word itself unto them in the evidence and demonstration of the Spirit."[27]

The problem with Augustine's approach is not necessarily his view of the miraculous, despite our misgivings about certain conclusions he makes concerning them. It is that he elevates objects such as relics and shrines to an unbiblical position for the sake of then proposing that the

---

27 John Owen, *The Work of the Spirit* (1853; reprint Carlisle, PA: The Banner of Truth Trust: 1967), 103.

miracles which are seemingly related to them are means to convert the lost or to argue for the truth of Christianity. He seems to think that the end justifies the means. If people are converted through such things, they are valid. We see here why the regulative principle must not only guide our worship services, but also our evangelism methodologies. Scripture demonstrates that gospel proclamation is how people get converted, whether it is from a pulpit, at work, at home, or with neighbors or strangers. We don't need to add to this method, even if it would mean more "success" in the eyes of our spiritual opponents or friends.

Augustine's Evangelistic Preaching

The Augustine of contemporary scholarship is a philosophical theologian and pastor. What is missing from this picture is Augustine's prowess as an evangelistic preacher. About Augustine's preaching, his contemporary and fellow minister describes him as follows: "Those who read what Augustine has written in his works on divine subjects profit greatly, but I believe that the ones who really profited were those who actually heard him and saw him preach in church."[1] This statement has been corroborated by his enemies also. A Manichean teacher once called Augustine "a consummate orator and a god of eloquence."[2] Augustine preached four to five times a week,[3] which was unique among ministers of his time. Unlike most bishops, he distinguished himself by devoting himself to the ministry of preaching.[4] He was "frenetically

---

1 Possidius, *Life of Augustine*, Ch. 31.
2 Secundius, as found in *Augustine In His Own Words*, Ed. William Harmless (Washington D.C.: Catholic University of America Press), 122.
3 *Works of Augustine*, 13.
4 Peter T. Sanlon, *Augustine's Theology of Preaching* (Minneapolis, MN: Augsburg Fortress, 2014), xix.

active," as we have seen, but never too busy to preach.[5] Moreover, much of his preaching was evangelistic. He preached not to entertain, but to persuade. His sermons seem to always be aware of unbelievers and nominal Christians among the congregation.

William Harmless has captured the setting of Augustine's church service in his book, *Augustine in His Own Words*: "The first thing one would have noticed upon entering Augustine's church was the flicker of flames from small oil lamps, filling the interior with a golden glow...There were no pews. The congregation stood, men on one side, women on the other. Services could draw packed audiences. 'The great numbers,' Augustine once noted, 'crowd right up to the walls; they annoy each other by the pressure and almost choke each other by their overflowing numbers.'"[6]

Augustine's evangelistic preaching can only be understood in the context of his view of the church. Although Augustine saw the church as Christ's "true body," he recognized there would simultaneously exist in it a type of "dilution" or corruption, since there would always be the presence of sinners in its midst. The church must "admit the possibility—the need—for tolerating sinners within it until the end."[7] The church as an "eschatological community" is always growing, meaning true believers will continually be brought into it. The church is "simultaneously the medium in which and through the instrumentality of which this growth takes place, and its final, heavenly outcome."[8] And yet, until the eschatological fulfillment, there will always be an element of the profane among its members. "In truth, these two cities are entangled together in this world, and intermixed until the last judgment

---

5 Ibid, 13.
6 *Augustine In His Own Words*, Ed. William Harmless (Washington D.C.: Catholic University of America Press), 122-123.
7 Markus, *Saeculum*, 117.
8 Ibid, 119.

effect their separation."⁹ This is why there is a need for evangelistic preaching, even in the churches. This is the motive behind so many of Augustine's sermons which have an undoubtedly evangelistic tenor to them. This is also why he was compelled to preach far more than his contemporaries. He was burdened to see the lost saved. He was burdened to bring good news to them.

Augustine's Sermons

Reading Augustine's sermons is quite different from seeing and hearing them in person, as we can imagine. Augustine himself never used notes when preaching, nor did he write out any text before his sermon. He prepared "by prayer and study" and then preached as the Lord would lead. This is why his sermons can seem disjointed at times. However, as we have already seen, this also allowed for more spontaneous redirection as the occasion called for, as was the case when he preached against the Manicheans and consequently one of them was converted.[10] His sermons were recorded in shorthand by stenographers known as notorii, then passed down to us through the centuries.[11]

As William Harmless reminds us, "the texts preserve only a faint residue of his living speech. What has been lost is the very thing that gave his speech its dynamism: the cadence of delivery, the accents and pauses, the gestures and facial expressions." Anyone who has read the sermons of George Whitefield has experienced a similar deflation. Having heard of the power and pulpit mastery of Whitefield, when we come to his sermons, we find something much different. They are good. They read well. But it is apparent we are missing the zest of what made

---

9 *City of God*, 1.35.
10 See chapter 3 of this book.
11 *Augustine In His Own Words*, Ed. William Harmless (Washington D.C.: Catholic University of America Press), 124.

Whitefield so special to his hearers. In a sense the same can be said of Augustine. In another sense, at least to this author, the spontaneity and punch of Augustine's sermons typically still come through.

Augustine's sermons often read like something from the Great Awakening era. They are lively. The evangelistic thrust is unmistakable. For example, in a sermon called "On the Ten Strings of the Harp," Augustine notes "all the sinners and lovers of this world are delighted to hear the Lord is merciful and compassionate," but they aren't so excited that he is also "true."[12] If they had only heard he is merciful and compassionate, but not true, "you would already be devoting yourselves to your sins with a feeling of security and impunity and freedom." He adds, "If anyone tried to scold or frighten you with some good advice about God, you would ask 'Why are you trying to scare me about our God?'" But it was for this reason that God made sure to inform them He was also true. "Thus he ruled out the smugness of presumption and prompted the anxiety of sorrow for sin." From there Augustine discusses the nature of God. He is just, and "there's nothing you can bank on when he comes, no false witnesses you can call that he will be taken in by, no tricky lawyers getting around the law with their clever tongues, nor will there be any way for you to fix it so that you can bribe the judge." Augustine then asks his hearers, "So what do you do before a judge like that, whom you can neither bribe nor deceive?"

This is the introduction to a sermon that will soon launch into an analysis of the ten commandments and whether his hearers have kept them. He will begin by reminding his hearers that death is always a moment away, so it is necessary to listen with sobriety. "Be assured of old age, if you can. But who can be? From the moment people begin to be able to live, they are also able to die, aren't they?...Since death

---

12 Sermon 9.1.

must be expected every day, make it up with your adversary while he is with you on the road." He tells his hearers that, for the lost, "the word of God" is the adversary. "It commands things against the grain which you don't do."[13]

Throughout the sermon Augustine is very aware that he may be disliked for such a message, but he is resolved to preach it anyways. "I am afraid that I too may be some people's adversary because I am speaking like this. Well, why should that bother me?...Whether they want me to or not, I'm going to say them. The one who tells you to behave is the same as the one who tells me to speak." He also speaks of the husband who is upset with him for saying adultery is evil, since many in his congregation were guilty of such a sin. Augustine compares himself to the doctor who, for the good of his patient, doesn't take into consideration the wishes of his sick patient. "If the doctor took any notice of sick people's wishes he would never cure them." Later he says, "Think of sick people. I am only hating your fevers, or rather the word of God in me is hating your fevers. This is why you should come to an agreement."[14] In other sermons he will make frequent reference to Christ the physician. He refers to himself as "a man strumming the ten-stringed harp," a reference to the ten commandments, and he harps on the commandment of adultery the most because "it's on this note that I see the whole human race fallen flat on its face. I'm going to pluck this string constantly."

The most shocking section of the sermon, at least for modern sensibilities, is when Augustine states, "God doesn't love you as you are, he hates you as you are. That's why he is sorry for you, because he hates you as you are, and wants to make you as you are not yet...God hates you as you are but loves you as he wants you to be, and that is why he

---

13 Ibid, 9.3.
14 Ibid, 9.10

urges you to change. Come to an agreement with him, and begin by having a good will and hating yourself as you are." Again, "Let this be the first clause of your agreement with the word of God, that you begin by first of all hating yourself as you are. When you too have begun to hate yourself as you are, just as God hates that version of you, then you are already beginning to love God himself as he is."[15] This idea of self comes up in other sermons, as well. When preaching on self-denial, Augustine remarks, "Learn to love yourself by not loving yourself."[16] He asks, "What does denying himself mean? He mustn't rely on himself, must realize he is merely human, and pay attention to the prophetic dictum, Cursed be everyone who places his hope in man (Jer. 17:5)."[17] Such statements were received in Augustine's day in a way similar to what we would expect in ours. Augustine would preach it anyways. "He must disengage himself from himself, but not in a downward direction. Let him disengage himself from himself in order to stick to God."[18] Augustine's robust view of man allows him to recognize the evils of self-love. His robust view of preaching gives him the impetus to say it.

Like the great evangelistic preachers who would follow, he often dramatized hypothetical responses in his sermons.[19] For instance, portraying a person who delays response to the gospel, Augustine asks, "'What's the hurry? I will mend my ways tomorrow,' they say." But "today is not standing still for you," he responds.[20] "Every argument with them is about putting things off…Tomorrow I will straighten myself

---

15 Ibid, 9.9.
16 Ibid, 96.2.
17 Ibid.
18 Ibid.
19 See Dr. Paul Sanchez's paper, "A Zealous Evangelist: Augustine's Urgent Call for Faith and Repentance" (unpublished paper), Oct. 29, 2015.
20 Dolbeau 14, *Works of Augustine*, III/11, 88–89.

out; I'll change; I'll mend my ways."[21] But no one knows what each day might bring. No one is promised tomorrow. And for the nominal Christian whose assumed salvation excuses them to live in sin, Augustine snorts they will perish "out of hope."[22] Those who claim God is unjust since sin is inevitable also "perish out of despair."[23] He warns, "The perverse have no reason to be displeased with Him," because God is good—and so is His judgment.[24]

Augustine's solution is simple: "Do not delay being converted to the Lord."[25] God's wrath is coming, and no one will be saved except those who cling to the gospel in faith and repentance. God has promised forgiveness, but he has not promised tomorrow.[26] When preaching on Luke 13:10-13, "Unless you repent, you will all likewise perish," Augustine warns his hearers "All bad, iniquitous people, all incorrigible, criminal miscreants, lovers of the world, lewd and worthless fellows, unless they repent, die likewise."[27]

He frequently addresses his hearers in the second person plural, which even today is a hallmark of evangelistic preaching. He often dialogues in his sermons with biblical figures such as Paul and John the Baptist, allowing the congregation to eavesdrop on the conversation. Evangelistic preaching entails a rooting up of the congregation's self-deceit. Augustine's ability to plumb the psyche of man, and especially sinful man, is a strength that he conveys in nearly every sermon. Thus, his impact on the lost is unsurprising. "With him the reader [or hearer] feels himself addressed at a level of extraordinary psychological

---

21 Dolbeau 14.1.
22 Dolbeau 14, *Works of Augustine*, III/11, 91.
23 Ibid, 91.
24 Dolbeau 14.9.
25 Dolbeau 14, *Works of Augustine*, III/11, 91.
26 Ibid, 92.
27 Ibid, 96.

depth and confronted by a coherent system of thought."[28]

The Free Offer of the Gospel

Also like the great evangelists who would follow, he preached what would later be called the free offer of the gospel. Augustine tells the unbelievers in his audience to "listen to the voice of God, not your own: 'Desperate soul, start hoping again'...God says, 'On whatever day the wicked and godless person is converted, I will forget all their iniquities.'"[29] God's mercy is great, and His arms were open to all. No one was too far gone in their sin to repent.[30] Augustine cites Ezekiel 18:21–22 as proof that God will forgive a sinner if he repents: "But if the wicked will turn from all his sins that he hath committed, and keep all my statutes, and do that which is lawful and right, he shall surely live, he shall not die. All his transgressions that he hath committed, they shall not be mentioned unto him: in his righteousness that he hath done he shall live." Referring to this text, he exclaims, "Read and believe. You were sitting on the river bank or you were carrying a noose around in your despair...Come back; you do have something to live on. Here is God's bread: 'I do not desire the death of the godless, so much as that he may turn back and live.'"[31] God has left no grounds for complaint. The gospel declares forgiveness of sins for those who have faith and repent. "What more can I say? Repent. You're a catechumen; repent and you will be renewed. You're a bad, baptized person, not badly baptized; repent and you will be healed."[32]

John Calvin would later quote Augustine to defend the doctrine of the two-dimensional depiction of God's will, or the so-called "two

---

28 Henry Chadwick, *Augustine: A Very Short Introduction* (Oxford Press, 1986), 4.
29 Dolbeau 14.8.
30 Dolbeau 14, *Works of Augustine*, III/11, 92.
31 Dolbeau 14.8, *Works of Augustine*, III/11, 93.
32 Dolbeau 14, *Works of Augustine*, III/11, 93.

wills of God."[33] God desires the salvation of all people and yet He elects and predestines only a specific number of persons to be saved. This is why the general call of the gospel must not be abandoned even by those who hold to a view of Scripture that is robustly predestinarian. There is a sincere offer of salvation to lost persons everywhere, as seen in Scripture (Ezek. 13:23, 33:11; 1 Tim. 2:4; 2 Pet. 3:9). But there is also found in Scripture the unmistakable fact that God alone chooses who will be saved (Eph. 1:4; John 15:16; Rom. 8:28-30, Rom. 9:16). In his *Institutes*, Calvin quotes from Augustine to solidify this necessity of the universal call of the gospel to all lost people, not only the elect: "For as we do not know who belongs to the number of the predestined or who does not belong, we ought to be so minded as to wish that all men be saved.' So shall it come about that we try to make every one we meet a sharer in our peace."[34] As we have already seen in previous chapters, such a view is the orthodox position of historic Reformed theology, and it was certainly Augustine's as well.

Later in Augustine's life, he became so formidable as a debater that many groups were unwilling to engage him. Although Augustine would call for meetings with religious foes for the purpose of debate and explication of doctrine, it became apparent that groups such as the Donatists were avoiding him. So Augustine turned to preaching, but not just in Hippo. He would travel to places like Carthage for the purpose of preaching against leading opponents who weren't there, but whose followers would have been. "He would rhetorically construct his opponents' position and demolish it. These sermons also would be recorded and circulated."[35]

At times Augustine's preaching makes havoc of what we would call

---

33 See Calvin's debate with Dutch Roman Catholic, Albert Pighius.
34 Calvin, *Institutes*, 2:964.
35 Six-Means, *Augustine and Catholic Christianization*, 88.

a law-gospel distinction. Although "of all the Fathers of the Church Augustine is undoubtedly the one who speaks most often and most extensively of Christ in his sermons,"[36] there is an occasional emphasis of almsgiving and other works which comes across as moralistic. However, he is also quick to point out that almsgiving is useless when done with wrong motives. Works don't "wipe clean" the slate of sin. Works don't save. What the sinner needs in order to be saved is an internal change which in turn leads to external change, not the other way around. "If you were an adulterer, stop being an adulterer; if you were a fornicator, stop being a fornicator; if a murdered, stop being a murderer...Or do you really think these things can be wiped off the slate by daily almsgiving unless they cease to be committed?"[37] In another sermon he explains it this way: "Each one of us, brethren, also undergoes a change from 'the old' to 'the new man': from an infidel to a believer: from a thief to a giver of alms."[38]

Homiletics with Augustine

Augustine was aware of the importance of preaching and the awesome weight of its responsibility. "How much safer a place you are standing in by listening than I am by preaching." Elsewhere he groans, "I am driven by the dread I feel, knowing that I am going to have to give an account to the Lord himself for you all."[39] The reality of a pending judgment was frightening news for sinners, but Augustine also senses the weight of his own stewardship for the people to whom he preaches. "So if you preach, do it deliberately, out of love, not casually and by the

---

36 M. F. Berrouard, "St. Augustine et le ministère de la predication. Le theme des anges qui montent et qui descendent," *Recherche augustiniennes* 2 (1962), 488 as cited in Pellgrino's introduction, *Sermons* III, 1, 60, n. 34.

37 Sermon 9.18.

38 Ibid, 44.

39 Dolbeau Sermon *114B, Works of Augustine*, III/11, 114.

way."[40]

The calling of the preacher demands urgency. He must be entirely absorbed in the work. Moreover, he must be a man devoted to prayer: "The preacher should be a person of prayer before he is a speaker of words. As the hour when he is to speak approaches, before he uses his tongue, he should raise his parched soul to God that he may gush forth what he has drunk in and pour out what has filled him up…Who knows what is appropriate for us to say or for our audience to hear except the One who sees 'the hearts of all'? And who can make sure that we say what we should say and in a way we should say it except the One in whose 'hands are both we and our words'? Anyone who wants to be knowledgeable and to teach should learn everything necessary… Yet as the hour for preaching nears, he should consider what the Lord says for a good frame of mind: 'Do not be anxious about what to say or how to say it; for what you are to say will be given you in that hour.'"[41]

In *On Christian Doctrine*, Augustine tells us of the threefold requirement of public speaking which he takes from Cicero. The orator must teach, delight, and persuade. "A speech should be varied and draw on all three styles insofar as this can be accomplished gracefully."[42] In order to teach well, the orator must have his listener's attention, which happens by the listener being "delighted." Delight doesn't mean be funny or trivial, but rather engaging—both in substance and manner. But the hearer must also be persuaded to not only listen to the teaching, but to put such teaching into practice.[43] This is chiefly what the orator must aim for. In this sense, Augustine is the precursor for what would later be called experiential preaching.

---

40 Sermon 101.9.
41 *On Christian Doctrine*, 4.15.32.
42 Ibid, 4.22.51.
43 Ibid, 4.12.27.

That those who try to convince people of falsehoods should know how to use their opening remarks to win over the audience's goodwill, to grab their attention, to make them receptive, while defenders of truth do not know how to do this? That those who argue falsehoods know how to do so cogently, clearly, and plausibly, while defenders of truth make their case in ways too boring to listen to, too convoluted to understand, and in the end, too distasteful to believe?…That those others, in order to move to or force their hearers' minds into error by their speaking, know how to inspire fear, to move hearers to tears, to get them laughing or burning with enthusiasm, while truth-tellers seem slow and tepid and end up putting people to sleep? Who is so insane as to think that's right? The capacity for eloquence—so effective in persuading people to either right or wrong—is available to both sides. Why then do the good not acquire the skill to battle for truth, if the wicked, in order to win unjustifiable and baseless cases, usurp it on behalf of injustice and error?[44]

Augustine believes it more critical that a preacher is wise and truthful than eloquent.[45] He must be clear. Augustine would agree with the Puritans' desire for "plain preaching." It is no wonder William Perkins has acknowledged his influential homiletics work, *The Arte of Prophesying,* was influenced by Augustine's own work on homiletics.[46] Both ministers emphasize that the preacher is not a politician. He is not a rhetorician. He is a minister of the gospel. His words have the power to influence person's souls for eternity. "But we must beware of

---

44 Ibid, 4.2.3.
45 Ibid, 4.5.7.
46 Ann-Stephane Schäfer, *Auctoritas Patrum? The Reception of Church Fathers in Puritanism* (Mainz: Peter Lang, 2012), 227.

the man who abounds in eloquent nonsense, and so much the more if the hearer is pleased with what is not worth listening to, and thinks that because the speaker is eloquent what he says must be true."[47] The task of preaching is grave. The responsibility is overwhelming. It is more important for the preacher to be biblical than to possess the art of rhetoric.

During Augustine's early days as a presbyterate—before he was a bishop—he wrote to the current bishop to reform drunken celebrations on saints' days by preaching more sermons "with scriptural explanations so that the people had a clearer understanding."[48] Throughout his ministry, this would be his chief approach to reform, again demonstrating why he preached as often as he did.

We see this in Augustine's development as a preacher as he spent more time doing it. An extensive survey of Augustine's sermons has shown that, in Augustine's early years, he demonstrates a high level of rhetorical flair. It likely would have been lost to his hearers. Over time he becomes more extemporaneous and "plain." The audience was undoubtedly less educated than he was, so wisely Augustine adapted his style accordingly.[49] This is an important quality of Augustine the evangelist. He knows his crowd. He knows how to adapt without compromising his message. He is willing to condescend intellectually and even stylistically for the sake of the souls to whom he preaches. In a letter to Simplician he admits, "Educated Christians like myself expect God's grace to prefer people of greater natural ability, higher standards of behavior, and superior education in the liberal arts. In fact, God mocks my expectations."[50]

47 *On Christian Doctrine*, 4.5.7.
48 Chadwick, *Augustine of Hippo: A Life*, 70.
49 Steven M. Oberhelman, *Rhetoric and Homiletics in Fourth-Century Christian Literature* (Atlanta: Scholars Press, 1991), 108-109.
50 *DS* 1.2.22.

Augustine's "secret" was his ability and desire to read his audience as he preached and to respond accordingly. He explains that because the hearers don't have the ability to ask questions and stop the preacher during the sermon, the preacher must "be especially attentive to come to the aid of the silent."[51] The preacher can do this by observing how the audience is reacting to his sermon. "An enthusiastic crowd, eager to learn, usually shows by its behavior whether it has understood things, and until it does, the speaker needs to keep going over and over whatever he is discussing in a whole variety of different ways."[52] Here Augustine criticizes those who "have previously prepared and memorized [their sermon] word-for-word," since they won't be able to cater their sermon to the congregation's understanding or perhaps misunderstanding. This is not always the case, of course, since those who use notes are still able to gauge their audience and even redirect at times, but Augustine's point is insightful since it comes from an experienced preacher and, before that, a respected professor of oratory.

The preacher should not be wooden or oblivious to the responses of his audience. His job is "to teach what is right and to refute what is wrong, and in the performance of this task to conciliate the hostile, to rouse the careless, and to tell the ignorant both what is occurring at present and what is probable in the future." To do so, he must be aware of whether his audience is hostile, careless, or ignorant. And in evangelistic fashion, he observes that if his hearers need to be roused, and particularly if they are doctrinally sound but listless in duty, the preacher must "bring their feelings into harmony with the truths they admit." In such a scenario he commends "a greater vigour of speech... Entreaties and reproaches, exhortations and upbraidings, and all the other means of rousing the emotions, are necessary." Again, we see here

---

51 *On Christian Doctrine*, Book 4.10.25.
52 Ibid.

the foundation of experiential preaching.

Augustine the Preacher

Despite Augustine's relish for preaching, he doesn't seem to idolize it. He seems to live chiefly for communion with Christ and service to His people. The preacher must above all else be a man who lives a holy life. He acknowledges that "whatever may be the majesty of the style [of preaching], the life of the speaker will count for more in securing the hearer's compliance."[53] Success as an evangelist depends as much on a genuine walk with the Lord as it does command, eloquence and proper exegesis in the pulpit.

The more one reads Augustine's sermons the more it becomes clear how seriously he took his calling, and yet how much he enjoyed it. Augustine's audiences were noisy. They would boo, shout in protest, or even jeer him out of the pulpit.[54] He would handle it in stride, however, as is apparent in another of his sermons where the applause of his audience catches him by surprise. "Alluring is the world, but more alluring is the One by whom the world was made. [*The congregation here begins cheering.*] What? What did I say? What is there to start cheering about? Look, the problem in the text has only just been laid out, and you've already started cheering."[55]

Even more so than a writer, Augustine was made to preach. But he didn't preach just anything. Perhaps more than anyone of his time, he preached Christ and Him crucified. The spirit in which Augustine comes across as a preacher is very much in the mold of Jeremiah: "But if I say, 'I will not remember Him nor speak anymore in His name,' then in my heart it becomes like a burning fire shut up in my

---

53 *Of Christian Doctrine*, 4.27.
54 Sermon 359B (Dolbeau 2).
55 Sermon 96.23.

bones; and I am tired of holding it in, and I cannot endure it." (Jer. 20:9).

conclusion

Augustine's shortcomings as an evangelist are many when interpreted through the lens of our contemporary context. There is no excusing certain decisions he makes, despite the influence his culture and training had on such decisions. Augustine can at times be inconsistent, especially as it regards evangelistic pragmatism. He criticizes the Pelagians for stunning the will into action through a fear of hell but does something very similar when it comes to religious coercion. His taste for relics and the assumed miracles attached to them would certainly be problematic as the centuries unfolded—if not in his own day. Augustine was too liberal at times towards pagan philosophers, suggesting men such as Pythagoras had relied more on their own mind when discovering truths of the universe, and not the rites of pagan cults. "Perhaps, Christ, the Savior, without whom no one can be saved, revealed himself to them in some way or other."[1] He believes some changes "here and there" to the doctrine of ancient Platonists

---

1 *Essential Sermons*, 208.

would have induced them to become Christians, despite his biblical view of man's radical depravity written about elsewhere.[2] He suggests Christ liberated orators, poets, and good men who saw polytheism to be false—even though they had never heard the gospel.[3] At times he has a confused sense of the law and gospel, and his sermons can drift into moralism.

Perhaps his most woeful error is the influence he gives the sacraments in matters of salvation. Despite Augustine's robust view of salvation by grace alone, at times he is found proposing that salvation is only dispensed through the church and its sacraments. This is why Warfield has noted it is Augustine's doctrine of grace against his doctrine of the church that sets off the Reformation in the seventeenth century. Both views can be found in Augustine's *Confessions*. For instance, he writes, "You converted me to yourself so that I no longer sought…any of this world's promises," and again, "By your gift I had come totally not to will what I had willed but to will what you willed."[4] But in the same chapter Augustine ponders, "I recognized the act of your will, and I gave praise to your name, rejoicing in faith. But this faith would not let me feel safe about my past sins, since your baptism had not yet come to remit them."[5]

Augustine understands his conversion is entirely the work of God's grace and yet we see him flailing in the mire of inconsistency when he suggests conversion can't be consummated until he is a recipient of the church's sacraments. There is simply no escape for him here. The champion of sovereign grace, original sin, the radical depravity of man and predestination from the foundation of the world is staggered by a works-based prevarication. Thankfully the theological foundation he

---

2 *True Religion*, 4.7.
3 Letter 164.
4 *Confessions* 8.12, 9.1
5 Ibid, 9.4.

lays is enough for the Reformers to build upon centuries later, but it is also enough for the Roman Catholic Church to appeal to throughout the ages and into the present.

His evangelistic and theological shortcomings are vastly outweighed by his achievements, however. Perhaps the greatest achievement is his unwavering optimism in the power of God to save sinners and build up His church. When preaching on the difficulties of life, Augustine reminds his congregation it is God who preserves His people, both in saving them and bringing them into glory: "I myself will restore them, I myself comfort, I myself encourage, I myself make him promises, I myself will heal him if he believes."[6] Augustine's evangelism includes a constant emphasis on Christ as the One who saves. Fallen human beings have "a lust to dominate."[7] They deny any dependency on God. In contrast, Augustine places "Christ as the center of his view of religion and insists that Christ was the unique and necessary Mediator between God and humankind."[8]

Augustine's life is described as teaching and preaching the Word of God "in private and in public," and "with all confidence against the African heresies, especially the Donatists, Manichaens and pagans."[9] He did it through "books and extemporaneous sermons." According to Chadwick, even Augustine's more overtly theological works such as *On the Trinity* were written "for unconvinced but sympathetic readers."[10] He did it through letters, debates, and personal conversation. He did it by grounding his views in the Word of God. Peter Brown reports that Augustine's works include 42,816 citations from Scripture.[11] Au-

---

6 *Works of Augustine*, III/11, 113.
7 Brown, *Augustine of Hippo*, 326.
8 Ibid, 486.
9 Possidius, *Life of Augustine*.
10 Augustine of Hippo: A Life, 118.
11 Peter Brown, *Augustine of Hippo: A Biography*. Rev. ed. (Berkley, CA: University of California, 2000), 36.

gustine expected hermits, monks, and bishops to memorize their Bible, something Augustine did also. The result was "Christians, who did not keep silent but spread it abroad wherever they could, being filled with unspeakable joy and praise." Through the evangelistic labors of Augustine, the Christian church in Africa "began to lift its head, having for a long time lain prostrate, seduced, oppressed and overpowered, while the heretics were gaining strength."[12] Amazingly, "even the heretics themselves gathered together and with the Catholics listened most eagerly to these books and treatises which issued and flowed forth by the wonderful grace of God."[13]

Augustine recognized that the Bible teaches "salvation belongeth unto the LORD" (Ps. 3:8; Jonah 2:9) and is the result of divine election from before the foundation of the world, without any foreseen merit in the one elected. Apart from God's saving grace, founded on His unconditional election, men will never "choose" to follow Christ. Jesus told us, "A man can receive nothing, except it be given him from heaven" (John 3:27), which includes faith. Augustine realized God's grace is the only hope man has to be saved and, consequently, regarding evangelism, is the only hope we have when sharing the gospel. God must "rend the heavens" and "come down" (Isa. 64:1).

This is the legacy Augustine would leave to the church—the sovereignty of God in salvation, the power of God to preserve His sheep to the end, and an emphasis on Christ as the only way to be saved. What B. B. Warfield says about Augustine's work against the Pelagians could be said about his entire ministry: "Through the whole fabric of which runs the golden thread of the praise of God's ineffable grace."[14] In the last year of his life, Jerome sent a flattering letter to Augustine to

---

12 Possidius, *Life of Augustine.*
13 Ibid.
14 Warfield, "The Origin and Nature of Pelagianism," 32.

inform him that his ministry has "refounded the old faith" and that the attacks on him by heretics were testimonies to his success.[15] Augustine would also bequeath to the Reformed church the view that preaching is primary and must be evangelistic. He would lay the foundation for what would later become presuppositional apologetics. Warfield has claimed "it is Augustine who gave us the Reformation,"[16] and it is no accident Luther, Calvin and other magisterial Reformers deeply imbibed Augustine's evangelistic mindset, which helped spark what would prove to be the greatest revival since Pentecost—recalling the Church back to the doctrine of free grace and with it a more robust methodology of evangelism and missions.

Augustine was a man who made mistakes, but he was a man of immense talents who used them for the glory of God and the advance of the gospel. By the end of his life, he had seen his once pagan Thagaste become thoroughly suffused with the Christian faith: "All of you know it along with me: In this city there are many homes in which there is not a single pagan. There are no homes where there are no Christians to be found. And if one were to investigate it carefully, no home would be found where there are not more Christians than pagans."[17] This is the fruit of Augustine the evangelist, and the legacy he left to the church has proven to be just as tenacious. By God's grace, may men such as Augustine rise up again in biblical churches around the world, and especially the secular West.

---

15 Letter 195.
16 Warfield, *Studies in Tertullian and Augustine*, 322.
17 Sermon 302.19.

bibliography

Athanasius. *The Life of Antony and the Letter to Marcellinus.* Tr. Robert C. Gregg. Mahwah, NJ: Paulist Press, 1980.

Augustine. *City of God.* Tr. Marcus Dods. New York City: Random House, 1993.

Augustine. *Confessions.* Tr. Philip Burton. London: Everyman's Library, 2001.

Augustine. *Essential Sermons.* Ed. Daniel Doyle. Tr. Edmund Hill. New York, NY: New City Press, 2007.

Augustine. *On Christian Doctrine.* Tr. R. P. H. Green. Oxford: Oxford University Press, 1997.

Augustine In His Own Words. Ed. William Harmless. Washington D.C.: Catholic University of America Press, 2010.

Beeke, Joel and Paul M. Smalley. *Reformed Systematic Theology.* Vol. 2. Wheaton, IL: Crossway, 2020.

Berkhof, Louis. *Systematic Theology.* Carlisle, PA: The Banner of Truth, 1958

Bredenhof, Wes. *To Win Our Neighbors for Christ.* Grand Rapids: Reformation Heritage, 2015.

Brown, Peter. *Augustine of Hippo: A Biography.* Rev ed. Berkley, CA: University of California Press, 2000.

Brown, Peter. *Religion and Society in the Age of Saint Augustine.* London: Harper & Row, 1972.

Brown, Peter. *The World of Late Antiquity.* New York, 1971.

Chadwick, Henry. *Augustine of Hippo: A Life.* Oxford Press, 2009.

Chadwick, Henry. *Augustine: A Very Short Introduction.* Oxford Press, 1986.

Cochrane, Charles Norris. *Christianity and Classical Culture.* Oxford: Oxford University Press, 1942.

Companion to Study of St. Augustine. Ed. Roy W. Battenhouse. Oxford Press, 1955.

Eire, Carlos M. N. *Reformations.* New Haven, CT: Yale University, 2016.

Fortin, Ernest L. "St. Augustine." *History of Political Philosophy.* Ed. Levi Strauss. Chicago: University of Chicago Press, 1987.

MacMullen, Ramsay. *Christianity & Paganism in the Fourth to Eighth Centuries.* New Haven, CT: Yale University, 1997.

MacMullen, Ramsay. *Christianizing the Roman Empire.* New Haven, CT: Yale University, 1984.

Markus, R. A. *Saeculum: History and Society in the Theology of St. Augustine.* Cambridge: Cambridge University Press, 1970.

Metzger, Will. *Tell the Truth.* Downers Grove, IL: InterVarsity, 1981

Munkelt, Richard A. "Foreword" to *The Political and Social Ideas of St. Augustine.* New York, NY: Angelico Press, 2013.

Nicene and Post-Nicene Fathers. Series 1, Vol. 1. Ed. Philip Schaff. Grand

Rapids, MI: Christian Classics Ethereum Library.

Pelagius. *On Nature and Grace.*

Pelagius. *Defense of the Freedom of the Will.*

Possidius. *Life of St. Augustine.*

Sanlon, Peter T. *Augustine's Theology of Preaching.* Minneapolis, MN: Fortress, 2014.

Sanchez, Paul. "A Zealous Evangelist: Augustine's Urgent Call for Faith and Repentance." Unpublished Paper. Oct. 29, 2015.

Six-Means, Horace E. *Augustine and Catholic Christianization.* New York: Peter Lang Publishing, 2011.

Van Den Berg, J. A. *Biblical Argument in Manichean Missionary Practice.* Leiden: Koninklijke Brill NV, 2010.

The Confessions and Letters of St. Augustine. Ed. Philip Schaff. Grand Rapids: Christian Classics Ethereum Library.

Works of Saint Augustine: A Translation for the 21st Century. Ed. François Dolbeau. Hyde Park, NY: New City Press, 1990-2008.

Warfield, B. B. *Studies in Tertullian and Augustine.*

About The Greater Heritage

Mission

The Greater Heritage is a Bible teaching and Christian publishing ministry that equips Christians for an abundant life of service, personal spiritual growth and character development through the study of God's Word and the contributions of His people in the fields of art, literature and music throughout history.

What We Do

The Greater Heritage publishes original articles, books and Bible studies. The ministry also hosts a podcast. All of its books are made entirely in the USA.

Want to publish with us? Inquire at:

The Greater Heritage
1170 Tree Swallow Dr., Suite 309
Winter Springs, Florida 32708
info@thegreaterheritage.com
www.thegreaterheritage.com

Find more books and our latest catalog online at:

www.thegreaterheritage.com/shop

Lightning Source UK Ltd.
Milton Keynes UK
UKHW011003060223
416537UK00007B/1296

9 781953 855602